Data Analytics
&
Quality Management
Fundamental Tools

By Joseph Nguyen

Contents

Foreword

In the context of data analytics, the word "tool" is typically associated with a software tool, an app, or a computer system that helps users perform tasks more efficiently. In this book, however, the word tool conveys a more basic method for manipulating data such as in quality control and management to help users make decisions and take actions. When I was a young engineer at NUMMI (a joint venture between GM and Toyota), my manager instilled in me the habit of manually analyzing data even in complex problems that would typically require methods such as statistics and the design of experiments. One reason was that computer apps were less widely available than today, but also because it was Toyota's philosophy to understand the mechanics of the methods before using computer programs to speed things up. This practice served me well as a young engineer to learn the theory and the limitations of techniques in data analytics. Later when we used statistical tools we had to know what they told us about the data and what they did not. This book is a compilation of practical reflections on tools I used in Continuous Improvement, Operational Excellence, and Quality Engineering projects such as Six Sigma Black Belt and ISO 9001 audits of suppliers during the time I worked as a quality engineer and when I became an executive, demanding my engineers to do the same. Originally, I developed this course using videos and put it on Udemy, an online training platform to reach a broader industry audience. It includes the fundamental tools used in data analytics, such as seven traditional QC tools, the new seven quality management tools, and those I frequently used for data analysis and visualization. Many requirements from ISO 9001:2015, especially in sections 8, Operation, and 9, Performance Evaluation, can be met using these tools here.

I heard the mottos: "Data is truth!" or "Without data, you are only a person with an opinion!" or "In God we trust, everyone else brings data!". These bring home the importance of data in communicating with others. However, I later learned also that data alone does not give you total truth, only partial truth if some people intentionally withhold some unfavorable data or misuse the tools. The combination of data and the right tools is crucial in data analytics to obtain the important insights. In the meantime, companies are progressing and leveraging technology to develop new tools to maximize use of data. Data has moved from being collected randomly as needed to a more elaborate data gathering from existing sources. Analysis from a few samples of data using statistics, to big data with business intelligence, and now open AI on the internet. The advance of the computer provides a tremendous opportunity to see the big picture at a fast speed and in great detail.

The target audience for this book is data engineers, scientists, quality engineers, and those in management. The main emphasis in the book is the process, which I call data synthesis methods. It is like a carpenter who opens a toolbox with many tools but knows well which one to use for a particular task. When a tool is pulled out of the toolbox under the watchful eyes of a master, a student should demonstrate that he knows how to use it skillfully but, more importantly, that he chose the right tool.

This book has several demonstrations of using tools to solve everyday problems such as spaghetti chart, Individual moving range control chart, and graphs. At the end of each section is a simple quiz to test your knowledge. The answers to all the quizzes are in the appendix. The resource table in the appendix is the most valuable takeaway from this book. If you need help remembering something in this book, print a copy of the resource table and keep it near your desk. This knowledge sets apart the tyro from the seasoned engineer.

I encourage the readers to do the exercises outlined in this book and apply them daily. Think of this book as the first puzzle in a giant jigsaw puzzle you have embarked on to build your data analytics canvas. Each puzzle represents another experiential knowledge of know-why and know-how.

Section 1: Introduction

This book will teach you the fundamental tools commonly used in data analytics, particularly quality management, and continuous improvement (Kaizen). There are also exercises and quizzes to help you become acquainted with these powerful tools and a resource table for quick reference in the appendix.

You will learn.

1. The purpose of each tool, when to use it, and how to use it individually, how to synthesize them for complex problems.
2. Errors to avoid when collecting and analyzing data.
3. An overview of the relationship between these tools and data analytics, particularly business intelligence and big data.

You will receive a quick reference guide of all 17 tools. The goal is that by the end of this book, you will be a data engineer-in-training of these tools and be able to select the appropriate tools for your data analytics projects.

In this book, you will learn....

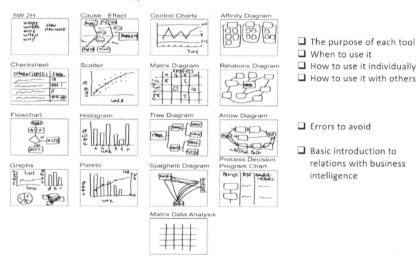

❏ The purpose of each tool
❏ When to use it
❏ How to use it individually
❏ How to use it with others

❏ Errors to avoid

❏ Basic introduction to relations with business intelligence

Introduction

The tool synthesis section is critical to distinguish between a novice and a master. Most tools can be used independently, but in complex situations, a set of tools is used in tandem to find solutions. For example, the following sequence of tools is used for a continuous improvement project: Checksheet, graphs, time series line chart, cause and effect diagram, Pareto diagram, and control charts.

When you have to present your solutions to others, such as your boss or clients, the tools you use to arrive at the answers may be questioned. These questions frequently check your confidence in your conclusions and the logic behind your choice. As a result, it is necessary to understand how to use the tools and why a particular tool or method was chosen. Communicating your findings and results for others to act on or approve necessitates logic and clarity. In this book, you will learn three synthesis methods.

Tool synthesis knowledge is critical to mastering the tools...

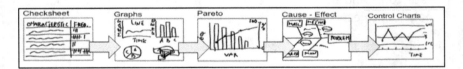

The seven traditional quality control tools are among the most powerful in a data analyst's or engineer's toolbox. They are checksheet, flowcharts, Pareto, scatter diagrams, cause and effect or fishbone, histograms, and control charts. However, tools are only a means to an end. Some tools are intended to serve a single purpose, whereas others serve multiple purposes. The seven traditional QC tools serve various functions. This book will teach you these seven tools so that by the end, you will have a thorough understanding of them and be able to use them correctly to improve processes and solve problems in the data analytics field, specifically in operations management, quality management, and continuous improvement.

In addition to the seven traditional tools, you will also learn the new seven management tools. They are affinity diagrams, relations diagrams, arrow diagrams, process decision program charts, systematic diagrams or tree diagrams, matrix diagrams, and matrix data analysis.

These tools are primarily concerned with non-numerical data, such as attributes nominal or ordinal data. More on these types of data can be found in the checksheet section. By the end of this book, you will be familiar with all of these tools.

In addition to these 14 tools, I chose three additional tools to make a robust toolbox for a data scientist and engineer. They are 5W 2H, spaghetti diagram, and graphs.

The section on avoiding errors includes a list of the top three errors for each of the seven traditional QC tools. These errors are based on my experience in my last 37 years working with these tools. Some countermeasures are provided to help you avoid making the same mistakes. Human errors and forgetfulness are part of human nature. However, willful errors are lies that can be caught only if one has insights into potential errors of these tools. Therefore, the adage "Data is truth!" is not always true. It depends on how data are presented and concluded.

The data analytics section, specifically on business intelligence and big data, connects these fundamental tools to the vast visualization tools available in software packages such as MS PowerBi. Statistics for small data and business intelligence for big data are not mutually exclusive; both have a place in the data analytics arsenal of a knowledgeable data engineer and scientist. This section will demonstrate the relationship between the seven traditional QC tools and data analytics, specifically in Business Intelligence and Big data.

Today, we can say without error that all companies, even start-ups, use data in their daily decision-making and problem-solving processes internally and externally as a strategy. This strategy comes from top leadership whose vision is to transform the company into data-centric decision-makers by taking full advantage of available data analytics software technologies. Data analytics comprises various strategies, tools, and methods to help companies run their business using data to deliver customer results. All departments' data are linked up and stored in data centers. Many software and tools applications are used in data analytics, such as business intelligence, big data, dashboards, machine learning, scorecards, artificial intelligence, cognitive computing, predictive analytics, and the Internet of Things IoT.

Companies use data in daily decision making…

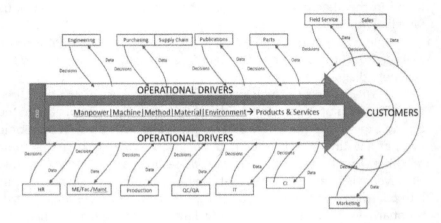

The diagram above is typical for a company with products and services that involve many departments. They design, engineer, manufacture, inspect, and sell to customers and provide support for human resources and external services. This broad picture shows that each department has its operational drivers to perform the functions they are responsible for, with data flowing across the organization to facilitate daily decisions. International standard requirements for a quality management system, such as ISO 9001:2015, are for companies like this one, where data availability is critical in every aspect of operation.

Top Leadership's Vision…

Large or small companies have top leaders who are well aware of their company's mission. Mission is nothing but the reason for the company's existence. DataXight's mission is to provide data analytics to biotech companies by knowledgeable software engineers and data scientists. Top management considers values necessary inherent characteristics that the company's culture should reflect as everybody embarks upon the mission to provide products and services to their customers. These are guideposts for behaviors. The vision follows with a view of where the company is going. In some companies, the vision statement is accompanied by the year the CEO envisions seeing it happen—for example, DataXight 2028 Vision is xxx. High-level goals usually articulate the vision. Strategies enable these goals; they provide more practical ways to reach the vision. From here, progress is reported in some scorecards as a pilot relies on the instrument panel and its many indicators in the cockpit to bring the plane to the right destination. Each functional department now develops and implements a plan to align with the company's vision and strategies. This process undoubtedly requires data and tools.

Companies use standard software packages to collect, store, and analyze data for daily decisions if available and meet their needs. For example, MS PowerBi software is a standard software package for PCs using Windows 365. PowerBi can handle very large checksheet or datasets, millions of rows and thousands of columns, and many data types, such as texts, numeric, date, attribute, and continuous. This is a considerable matrix diagram that contains many variables. ETL or extraction transform, and load converts it into a database that can be used for analysis.

Dataset is a Matrix Diagram

Thousands of columns

Data types

Millions of rows

Segment	Country	Product	Units Sold	Manufacturing Price	Month	Month Name
Enterprise	USA	Carretera	330 $	3.00	9	September
Midmarket	France	Carretera	490 $	3.00	11	November
Government	Germany	Paseo	360 $	10.00	10	October
Government	Germany	VTT	360 $	250.00	10	October
Government	USA	Paseo	380 $	10.00	9	September
Midmarket	Mexico	Paseo	380 $	10.00	12	December
Channel Partners	USA	Amarilla	270 $	260.00	2	February

The skillful user of PowerBi can select a visual from a vast menu of visuals to display for the dashboard and report. Many of these 17 tools taught in this book are visuals in the PowerBi standard toolbox and hundreds more in the AppSource that can be downloaded. In understanding and applying these 17 tools in this section, readers can select the right visuals for their dashboards and reports.

The guiding principles to master a technique are to learn, practice, and reflect. When it comes to practice, doing it by hand will provide insights into the workings of sophisticated apps or software packages.

Business Intelligence software is a powerful tool to leverage in many situations that deal with problem-solving or continuous improvement cases. It is a big hammer in the toolbox. But not all problems require a big hammer to solve. Therefore, in the arsenal of tools in the toolbox, Business Intelligence apps have their place, but many other tools must be ready to solve problems quickly. These 17 QC and management tools fall in the category of basic or fundamental tools in the toolbox. Once you master these tools, choosing visuals and building a dashboard in business intelligence software makes much more sense.

Introduction

Business Intelligence
and
Big Data

Problem Solving
and
Continuous Improvement Toolbox

So, let's start getting into each of the fundamental tools now.

1.1 Quiz 1: Test Your Knowledge

Question 1:

Why the adage "Data is Truth!" is not always true?

- ○ **Data contains errors**

- ○ **Data is only reflecting a small sample**

- ○ **Data can be interpreted wrong**

- ○ **Data can be manipulated**

- ○ **All of the above**

Question 2:

Why do we need the right tools for data analysis ?

- ○ **So that errors can be avoided**

- ○ **To build a good dashboard**

- ○ **To convert data into useful information**

- ○ **To maximize use of data**

Test Your Knowledge

What is the purpose of synthesizing tools?

○ **To use the right tools for the right purpose**

○ **To maximize the benefits of tools**

○ **To show the logic of arriving at a conclusion**

○ **All of the above**

Question 4:

Is checksheet used for tally count only?

○ **Yes.**

○ **No, Checksheet can be used for any type of data.**

Question 5:

Is Pareto the same as bar chart with bars arranged from highest to lowest frequency? dick

○ **Yes, they are the same only with bars re-arranged. The**

○ **No, they are different because Pareto diagram follows the 80/20 rules**

○ **No, they are different because Pareto diagram has percent cumulative line.**

Section 2: Seven Traditional Quality Control Tools

2.1 Flow Chart and Its Derivatives

A flow chart is a tool for visually documenting and analyzing a process. Flow charts describe a simple or complex process depending on the scope of the situation. The advantage of this tool is that it lists the facts in the logical sequence of a process, allowing the mind to grasp the big picture and visually grasp the opportunities for further analysis.

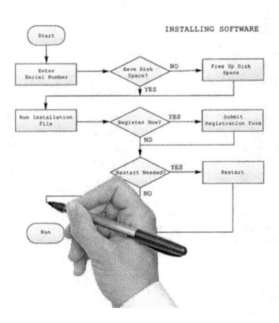

Many flow charts are used in various situations, but they all have five main types of information. They adhere to the SIPOC model, which stands for supplier, input, process, output, and customer. Each category can contain a variety of activities related to the details desired and the process's boundaries. For example, a supplier can be a single component or an entire manufacturing process. Similarly, for the customer, it can be as simple as a receiving point or as complex as how the customer handles the product after it is delivered, including feedback loops if the product is returned.

The following flow charts are commonly used for problem-solving and continuous improvement: spaghetti diagrams, swim lane flowcharts, process maps, and value stream maps.

Spaghetti Diagrams

Spaghetti diagrams, transportation, or workflow diagrams, depict people, materials, or information flow visually. This tool reduces movement and overprocessing waste, allowing the process to be streamlined and output faster. To create a spaghetti diagram, first create an overhead layout of the work area, including the current locations of equipment, materials, and people. List the steps of the process and connect the first step with an arrow pointing to the second step, and then continue with another arrow from the second step to the third, and then another arrow from the third to the fourth, and so on until all of the steps are connected with arrows. How to interpret the data: numerous arrows pointing to an object crisscrossing arrows indicate opportunities to reduce excessive movement for smoother flow.

SPAGHETTI DIAGRAM
(FLOW of MATERIALS, INFORMATION, PEOPLE)

LAYOUT

EQUIPMENT A

MATERIAL LOCATION 1

MATERIAL LOCATION 2

EQUIPMENT B

people

In the next section, I will demonstrate how to use this seemingly simple but powerful tool. This tool requires actual observation of the movement of people and materials.   For young engineers, "go and see" with our eyes is usually the mandate to use this tool. However, today, anyone can record a scene easily and play it back for study with a mobile phone, and many people can view the movements multiple times for the analysis of data.

Swim Lane Flowcharts

The "Who", as in who does what activities, is highlighted in the swim lane flowcharts. Each lane depicts the activities of a person, a department, or a company representative. The swim lane flowchart makes it simple to see who is responsible for what and how information and materials are linked to them.

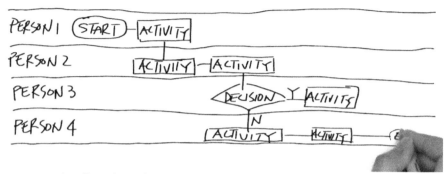

SWIM LANES

The flowcharts' contents comprise the process map. It is a tool for describing how something is made or how a customer is served. It typically has a beginning and an end, indicating the scope of the process under investigation. In the industry, symbols are used as a common language to understand the types of activities in the process quickly. Hundreds of customized symbols are available, and here are a few of the most common. The process map can be created in either vertical or horizontal format.

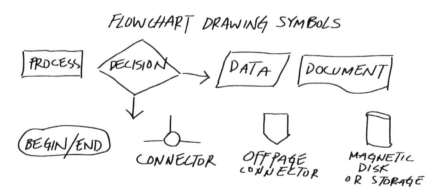

FLOWCHART DRAWING SYMBOLS

THESE SYMBOLS ARE THE COMMON ONES. CONSULT SPECIFIC INDUSTRY FOR OTHERS

Process Maps

Most process maps are drawn horizontally, but they can also be drawn vertically to scroll the information quickly. Either way will work as long as it meets the customers' needs.

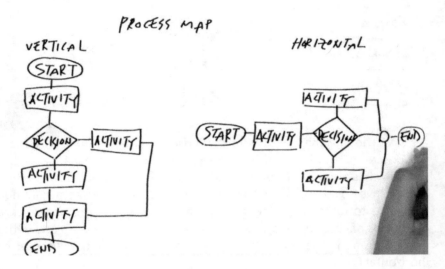

The value stream map is the most commonly used tool for studying and improving a process. It tracks the time it takes to make a product, from when it is ordered to when it is delivered to the customer. It visually depicts the flow of materials and information, as well as opportunities for improvement in the form of non-value-added activities such as waiting, moving materials, and excessive processing. The PCE, which stands for process cycle efficiency, is the primary indicator of value stream mapping. PCE is a percentage of total time spent on value-added activities in producing a product; the remainder is waste and is treated as an opportunity for improvement.

Value Stream Maps

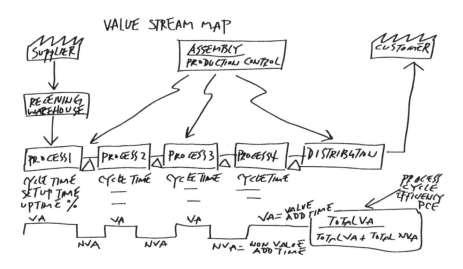

The value stream map begins with the SIPOC model, and the entire model is analyzed in detail for opportunities for improvement. However, the focus is typically on the P or Process, where value-added and non-value-added activities occur most frequently. Typically, the improvement in time measured as seconds or minutes is very small compared to the total time (or lead time) of the SIPOC. But this is not the goal. The goal is to compare the PCE before and the PCE after to see the percent improvement. And this can be great.

2.1.1 Demo of the Spaghetti Diagram in Cooking Breakfast in Less Than Five Minutes

In this section, you will see how a spaghetti chart is made and how to use it to improve a situation. Making breakfast in the morning is the situation. The issue is that it takes too long to prepare breakfast. Breakfast consists of a 12 oz cup of fresh coffee brewed from a coffee machine, three eggs cooked sunny side up with onions and salt in a pan, three links of sausage microwaved for 40 seconds, two slices of toast toasted in a toaster, a jar of jam, a fork, and a knife. (See illustration.) We'll start with a kitchen layout that shows where everything is kept, a step-by-step breakdown of how each item is made, and a spaghetti chart.

The goal is to cook this breakfast within 5 minutes each morning. The process we use for this improvement is as follows:

1. We study the requirements of this meal.
2. We record the baseline of how long it takes to cook it.
3. We map out the process using a spaghetti diagram to identify opportunities for improvement.
4. We improve and finally, confirm the new approach with the new time.

The situation:
It takes too much time cooking this breakfast

The goal:
Cooking breakfast within 5 minutes

The process:
1. Study the standard requirement of this meal
2. The current baseline, how long does it take to cook this breakfast normally
3. Map out the process of cooking breakfast using spaghetti diagram and charts and graphs
4. Improve the process
5. Check the new process and record the new time

Here is the standard requirement of the meal.

A 12 oz cup of coffee brewed from Keurig coffee machine
Three eggs cooked using butter in a frying pan, sunny side up with onions, a few sprinkles of salt
Three links of sausage microwaved for 40 seconds on a plate
Two slices of toast cooked in a toaster
A jar of jam
a fork
a spread knife

To study the process flow, we need the layout. On the right is the actual kitchen, and on the left is the layout.

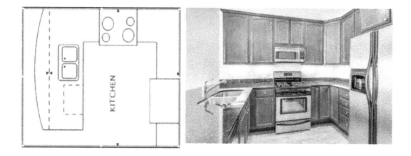

Then, we video-record the entire process from start to end. This video is the actual capture of each step involved in making this breakfast. Information from this video is playback, and each step is recorded on an Excel spreadsheet with the time element. Please watch the entire video[1] or speed up to the end if you would like. It takes 9 minutes and 29 seconds to make a complete breakfast.

---

[1] See YouTube video (https://youtu.be/H0lPdePlVKs)

Here is the beginning of mapping the spaghetti chart. The process is recorded on the left. Then the layout is brought back so that all locations of the equipment and materials used in this process are drawn in the layout.

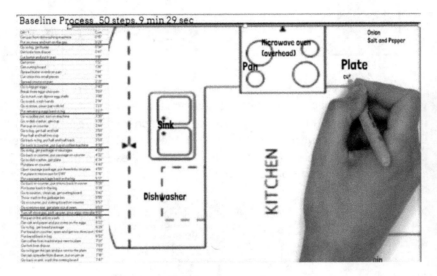

Once the chart is drawn, we look for opportunities for improvement. We see many trips to the refrigerator and too many walks to the dishwasher and sink across the kitchen. We see opportunities for simultaneous work or doing many things simultaneously from the process.

Flowchart and its Derivatives

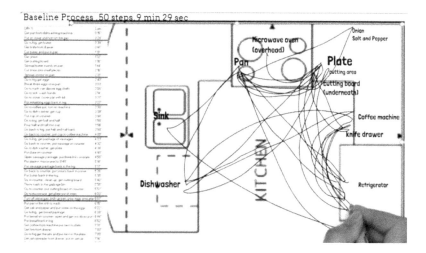

Baseline Process. 50 steps. 9 min 29 sec

Opportunities for Improvement

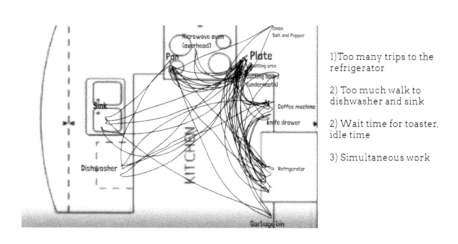

1)Too many trips to the refrigerator

2) Too much walk to dishwasher and sink

2) Wait time for toaster, idle time

3) Simultaneous work

Here is the improvement made for day 2 and day 3. The baseline has 50 steps, and it takes 9'29", day 2 it takes only 33 steps and 6'38", day 3 it takes the same number of steps, but the time was reduced to 4'45" which is less than 5 minutes. Our objective has been met.

We recorded another spaghetti chart from day 2 and compared it to day 1 and we see the chart is less busy around the refrigerator.

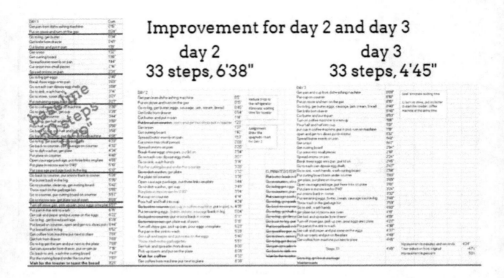

Improvement for day 2 and day 3

day 2
33 steps, 6'38"

day 3
33 steps, 4'45"

Spaghetti chart day 1

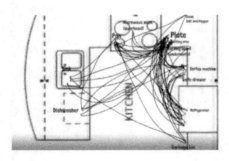

Spaghetti chart day 2

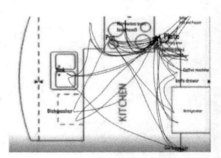

fewer trips to the
refrigerator

Challenge: Can you draw the spaghetti charts for day 2 and day 3? How different is yours to the one shown here?

2.2. Checksheets

Checksheets are data collection and organization tools. Checksheets are typically used to collect raw data to be converted into information. In this section, you will learn different types of checksheets and how to create and use the right tools for the appropriate tasks. Standard forms are designed to make it easy to collect and organize data.

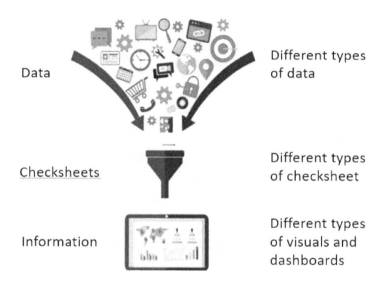

Data — Different types of data

Checksheets — Different types of checksheet

Information — Different types of visuals and dashboards

Let us first define the various types of data. Continuous data are measurements taken on a scale that can be infinitely divided. For instance: 2.3, 1.23, 20, 100.01. Attribute data, also known as discrete data, can be grouped into four categories: 1) count data or percentage data; 2) binomial attribute data are data with only two options, such as yes or no, pass or fail; 3) nominal attribute data has names attached to it, such as product A, B, C, D, etc. and 4) Ordinal attribute data, also known as ranking attribute data, contains data ranks such as exceptional, very good, good, average, fair, and bad. Continuous data is preferred over attribute data because it provides more information for statistical analysis.

TYPES OF DATA

CONTINUOUS
2.3
1.23
26.0
100.01

ATTRIBUTE → COUNT/%
↘ BINOMIAL: Y/N
↓ NOMINAL (NAMES)
↓ ORDINAL (ORDER/RANK)

Follow the PDCA process to create a checksheet meeting users' needs. The guiding principles for checksheet are that they are simple and easy to use.

Plan the checksheet by clearly stating the problem to be solved or improvement to be made. Define what or the characteristics you want to measure, the unit of measurement, when you want to measure it, the tool used to measure it, the name of the data collector, and what type of data is being measured (continuous, attribute, or locational data). The revision number is used to ensure the latest checksheet is used.

Create a simple checksheet by hand on a piece of paper. Data needs to be analyzed and converted into useful information later, so using a simple Excel spreadsheet as a checksheet is a common practice.

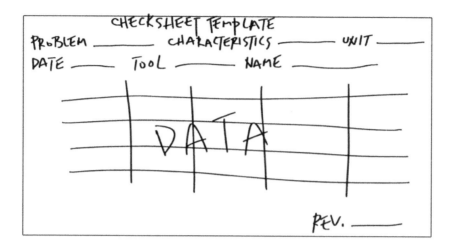

Test the checksheet by filling it out with a few measurements with some data to see if the format is appropriate for the task. If data analysis is to be done instantaneously, spaces on the checksheet may be required to record the analysis results. Control charts, for example, combine checksheets and results of means and standard deviations on the same piece of paper.

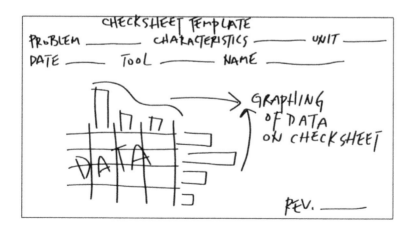

Checksheets

Checksheets are designed to collect time series data when we are interested in knowing the variations of the characteristics over time. The main elements of a checksheet include what or the features we want to measure when we want to measure it, and a matrix to enter data.

Checksheet to know variations over time (Time Series checksheet)

What we want to measure	When measurements are done				
	Time 1	Time 2	Time 3	Time 4	Time 5
Characteristic A	data	data	data	data	data
Characteristic B	data	data	data	data	data
Characteristic C	data	data	data	data	data
Characteristic D	data	data	data	data	data
Characteristic E	data	data	data	data	data

The basic checksheet for continuous data is shown. We want to measure the weight and height of a baby to see if the development is normal. We want to measure them at birth, and at one month interval after birth. Data is recorded in the provided excel spreadsheet.

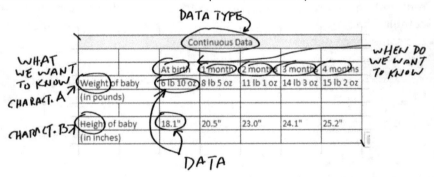

DATA TYPE

	Continuous Data					
		At birth	1 month	2 months	3 months	4 months
Weight of baby (in pounds)		6 lb 10 oz	8 lb 5 oz	11 lb 1 oz	14 lb 3 oz	15 lb 2 oz
Height of baby (in inches)		18.1"	20.5"	23.0"	24.1"	25.2"

WHAT WE WANT TO KNOW

CHARACT. A

CHARACT. B

WHEN DO WE WANT TO KNOW

DATA

Next is the example of a checksheet for attribute data for count and percentage. We want to know the population of the US and the percentage growth over the previous year.

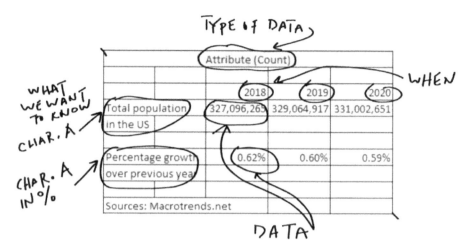

Next is the example of a checksheet for attribute data for binomial. We want to know the outcome of a coin toss whether it is head or tail each time a coin is tossed in succession. We denote 1 for yes, and 0 for no. Here the coin is tossed five times, and 3 times were heads, and 2 times were tails.

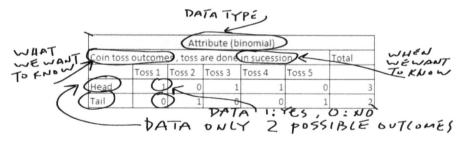

Next is the example of a checksheet for attribute data for nominal. Nominal is for names or text characteristics. We want to know the new readers admitted in the spring of 2021, their sex, country of origin, GPA, and race.

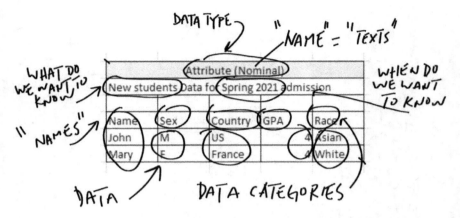

Another example is a checksheet for attribute data for ordinal. Ordinal is things arranged in an order or ranks. Here we want to survey the new car buyers of Toyota, Kia, and Mercedes, how likely they would recommend to their families or friends the car they just purchased. We use the ordinal scale of 0 to 10. 0 is never, 10 is very likely.

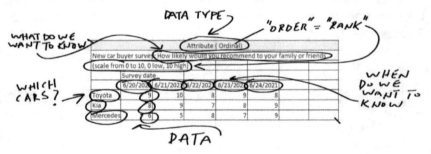

Data are also collected as a distribution, used for histograms. We use a combination of continuous data and attribute data. Continuous data of Grade Point Average or GPA and grouped into 6 histogram bars and attribute data as tally tick marks.

Checksheets

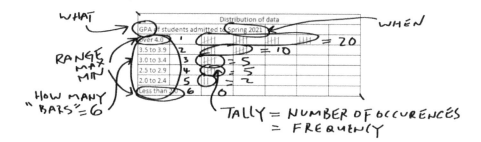

Checksheet are also designed to know the relationships between variables. Dependent variables are the outputs, and the independent variables are inputs. Data can be either continuous or attribute.

Here is an example of the checksheet to know the relationships between variables. We want to know each person named on the checksheet, their weights, whether they are married or not, how many children do they have, how much do they like to play golf using scale 0 to 10.

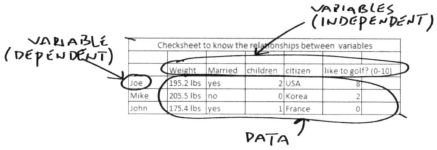

Checksheet for locational data is simply an image of the object used as checksheet. This type of checksheet is used to show where the characteristics are measured, and the data is recorded near or at the point of occurrence.

S = Scratch
D = Dent
C = Color Match
B = Bump

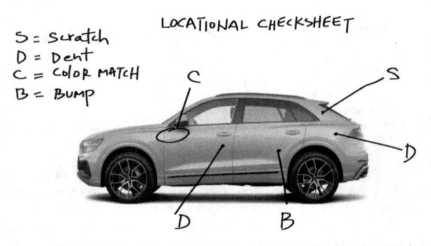

A checklist is a type of checksheet where the attribute binomial data is used for a list of characteristics. Here is an example of a checklist for grocery shopping.

For automatic data collection, data is collected and stored for analysis in large quantities. Data are filtered and sorted for analysis depending on the information required. Checksheet templates are used to design the type of data needed for automatic data collection.

Checksheets

In summary, checksheets are tools to collect and organize data. There are three types of data: variables, attributes, and locational. Checksheet are templates designed for manual data collection, so simplicity and ease of use is desired. Automated checksheets are used as depository of inputs to create automatic data collection.

2.3 Cause and Effect Diagram or Fishbone

The Cause-and-Effect or fishbone diagram is a chart that looks like a fish with bones and a head. The bones represent the many causes that affect the problem, defined as the head of the fish. The fishbone shows graphically the relationships between them. Typically, one fishbone diagram is used for one problem.

Fishbone Diagram

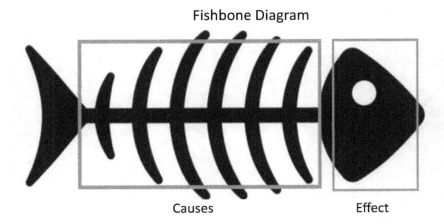

Causes   Effect

The cause-and-effect diagram is separate from the cause-and-effect matrix. Let me explain quickly here the difference between the two tools. The cause-and-effect matrix can have many effects and many causes. The relationships between causes and effects are not linear or not treated with the same importance value; some may be higher than others, and the matrix has columns to assign those values. The cause-and-effect diagram treats all causes with the same weights and has one effect.

Causes   Effects

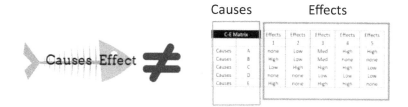

The fishbone and matrix can be used together, but usually, the fishbone is used first and the matrix after. Fishbone is a tool for brainstorming ideas for problem-solving or continuous improvement projects. For problem-solving, fishbone is used when immediate root causes are not known, thus the need for brainstorming to generate ideas as potential causes. Ideas from brainstorming sessions for possible causes are organized using a diagram of the main bones of a fish. Each bone represents a category of causes typically assigned the 5M's and 1 E of a process, which stand for man or people, machine, method, material, measurement, and environment.

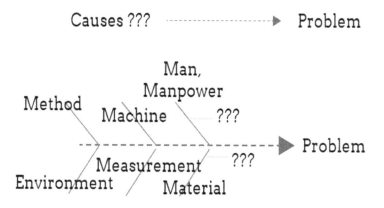

To create a cause-and-effect diagram, start with the problem or situation to be improved; this is the head of the fish or the "effect." Then, we generate the areas that we think are causes and connect them to the head by lines that represent the bones of the fish. Write ideas directly onto the fishbone chart or on a sticky note and transfer them to the fishbone. This method can be done individually or in a group. Group exercise is preferred since members can build on the ideas of others and reduce duplications. The key is to get all the ideas out on the chart. When too many causes clutter the chart, use another diagram to capture all the ideas.

To generate ideas, look at each category or the bone and ask: " Has anything here changed?" or "Has this been a cause of the past problems?". Once ideas are recorded on the fishbone, judge the correlation between each cause and the effect by giving each one a symbol. For example, an X over the cause means this cause does not affect the problem, a checkmark next to the cause indicates an effect, and a question mark is a cause that members are unsure about. This tool is used to judge the relationships between cause and effect. Later, a scatter diagram or correlation diagram is used to show whether the cause is a real cause, or it is only perceived.

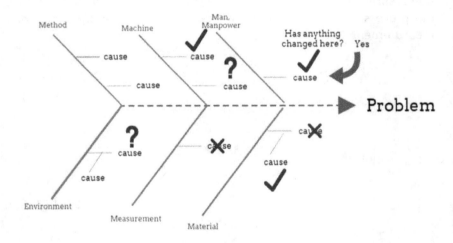

The fishbone diagram requires time to complete. Since time is valuable, as long as ideas continue to be generated, the brainstorming session must stop when thoughts are no longer developed. However, there are ways to be productive in generating ideas for fishbone diagrams. They rely on two known pieces of information: the problem, which is the head of the fish, and the main categories, which are the main bones of the fish. Ideas are attached to the bones. Therefore, the types or main bones must be well thought out to be productive in generating fishbone diagrams. The 5M and 1E are categories used in manufacturing, but as you can see here, the main types are different.

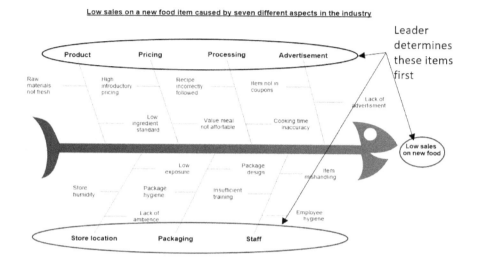

In summary, a fishbone diagram or cause and effect diagram is a tool to generate ideas as potential causes of a problem. Causes are generated by brainstorming or by experience. Causal ideas are grouped under specific categories such as people, machine, method, material, measurement, environment, etc. Finally, ideas are evaluated as having an effect, no effect, or uncertain. The key to a successful fishbone is to exhaust all possible ideas that can affect the problem under the guidance of an experienced person.

2.3.1 Fishbone Example and Exercises

In this section, you will learn how to use the cause-and-effect diagram tool to find causes for your problems. There are five examples and one template. Examples 1 and 2 are for your viewing. Use the blank template to create your fishbone diagrams, or use the ones provided for you to do examples 3, 4, and 5.

Example 1 is the cause-and-effect diagram of a worker who suffers from poor work-life balance. The four leading causes are personal life, work, balance, and others. As mentioned in the previous section, the leaders should list the leading causes before brainstorming to generate ideas. In this case, these four categories are provided to you. These categories were generated from work-life balance workshops, and the workshop participants gave the ideas. The internet provides a resource for concepts such as these. Then, this diagram filters relevant causes to your situation using the three symbols explained in the previous section: A check mark indicates relevance, an x indicates no cause, and a question mark indicates not sure. Example 1 shows the causes or reasons for his work-life imbalance. He is a workaholic; he considers work to be more important than anything else, he worries and does not manage time well. The following steps prioritize them and develop action plans to remedy these four causes.

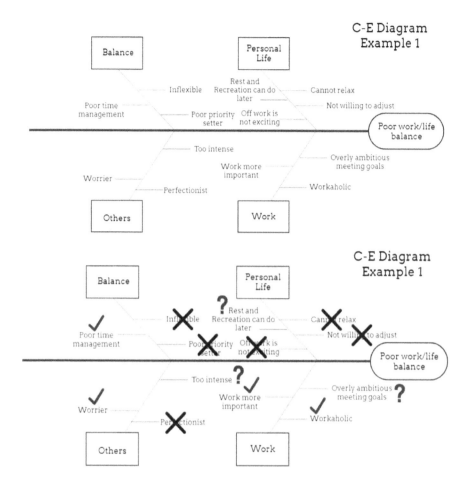

Example 2 is the cause-and-effect diagram of a person whose work output suffered poor quality. This diagram can be done by the person who just received the evaluation or by the supervisor who has a worker with this problem under him. The main categories are the work itself, the work standards, the worker, and others. Similar to example 1, the leading causes of poor quality of work output are provided here but can also be obtained by research on the internet. Then, the person who wants to improve his work output quality filters out what he thinks are the causes applicable to his situation. His work output has many errors and requires his supervisors and coworkers to fix them. He is new to the job and needs to be more skilled at what he is doing. Help was unavailable when he needed it, so he did his best. People say he is not customer-oriented or result-oriented, but he is still determined.   He works with his supervisor to improve output quality by improving his skills.

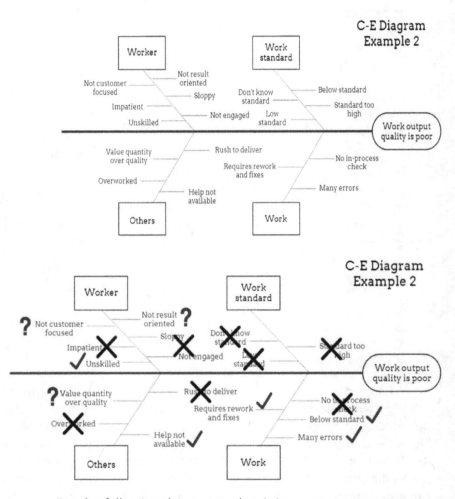

For the following three examples, it is your turn to create your fishbone diagrams. Follow these four steps and pause the section to give you time for each exercise. Each exercise should take about an hour to complete. Good luck, and we will see you in the next section.

Create Your Own Fishbone Diagrams

Step 1: Look at the diagram with the main categories provided

Step 2: Brain storm causes for each category, or research the internet and fill in the diagram

Step 3: Compare your diagram with the one provided

Step 4: Use check mark, X, or ? to identify relevant causes, not a cause and not sure on the diagram

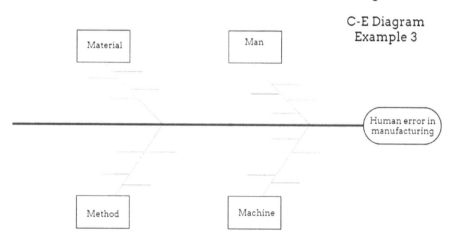

C-E Diagram
Example 3

Fishbone Diagram Example and Exercises

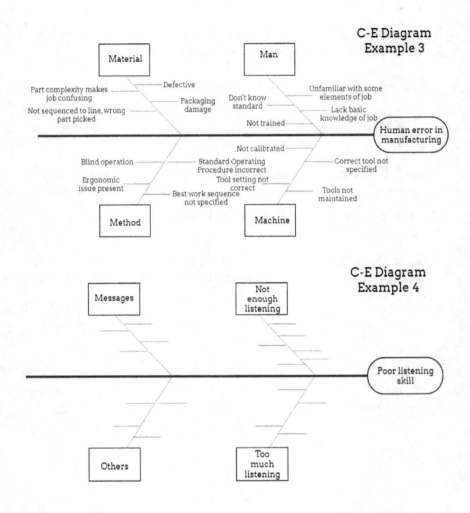

C-E Diagram Example 3

Material

Man

Defective
Part complexity makes job confusing
Packaging damage
Not sequenced to line, wrong part picked

Don't know standard
Unfamiliar with some elements of job
Lack basic knowledge of job
Not trained

Human error in manufacturing

Not calibrated
Blind operation
Standard Operating Procedure incorrect
Correct tool not specified
Ergonomic issue present
Tool setting not correct
Best work sequence not specified
Tools not maintained

Method

Machine

C-E Diagram Example 4

Messages

Not enough listening

Poor listening skill

Others

Too much listening

Fishbone Diagram Example and Exercises

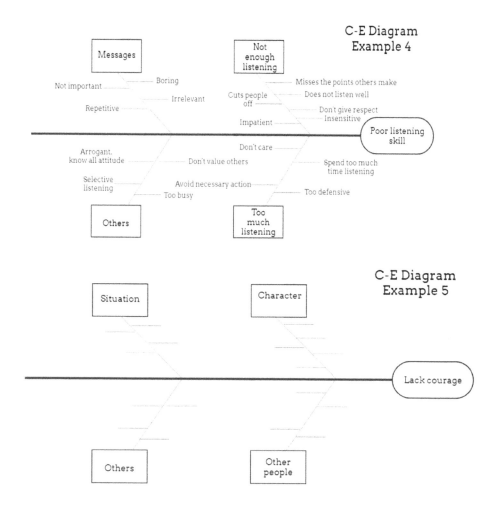

C-E Diagram Example 4

Messages

Not important — Boring
Irrelevant
Repetitive

Not enough listening

Misses the points others make
Cuts people off — Does not listen well
Don't give respect
Insensitive
Impatient

Poor listening skill

Arrogant, know all attitude — Don't care
Don't value others
Selective listening
Avoid necessary action — Spend too much time listening
Too busy — Too defensive

Others

Too much listening

C-E Diagram Example 5

Situation

Character

Lack courage

Others

Other people

Scatter Diagram

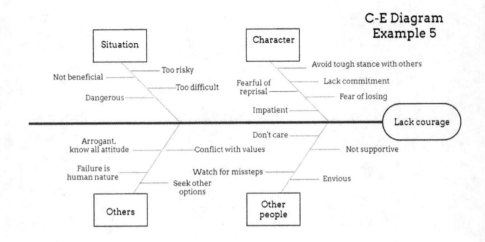

C-E Diagram
Example 5

Situation

Not beneficial ——— Too risky

———Too difficult

Dangerous———

Character

Avoid tough stance with others

Fearful of reprisal ——— Lack commitment

——— Fear of losing

Impatient———

Don't care———

Lack courage

Arrogant, know all attitude ——— Conflict with values ——— Not supportive

Failure is human nature — Watch for missteps ———

— Seek other options — Envious

Others

Other people

2.4. Scatter Diagram

The scatter diagram or scatter plot is a tool to show the relationship between two variables graphically and to confirm whether cause and effect exist. Two variables having a correlation or association does not necessarily mean there is always a cause-and-effect relationship between them. A very simplistic way to check if a cause-and-effect relationship exists graphically is when the cause increases the value, the effect value also increases. Similarly, when a cause decreases, the effect also decreases.

This relationship is called positive correlation. This method is only valid for cause and effect if the relationship is linear.

Four typical relationships or correlation patterns can be interpreted from a scatter diagram:

1. Two variables are not correlated when the data are scattered in a circle.
2. A positive correlation is when the data form a line from the bottom left to the top right direction in the diagram.
3. A negative correlation is when data start a line from the top left to the bottom right direction in the chart.
4. Complex correlation is when data form a nonlinear line, such as a curve.

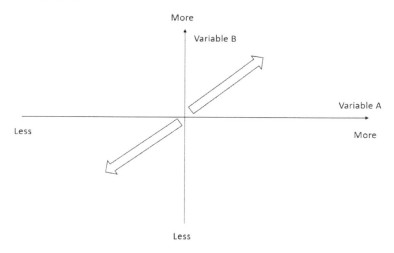

Scatter Diagram

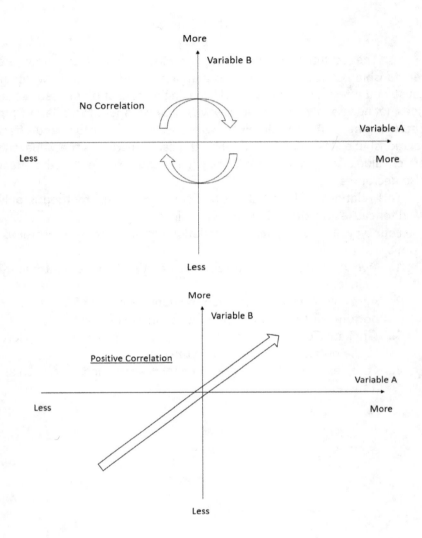

Scatter Diagram

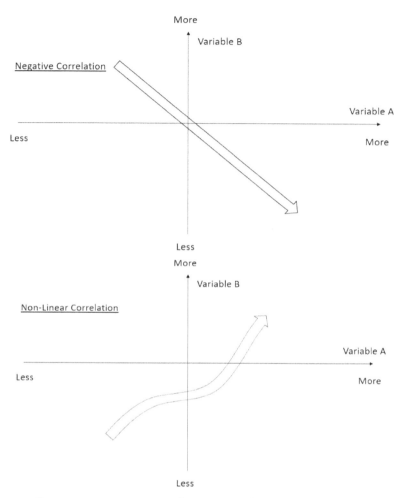

To construct a scatter diagram, collect data in pairs. In other words, each data point has two measurements of the variables being investigated. For example, we want to know if the length of a newborn baby correlates with his weight from birth to two years old. Each month, we collect one data point with two measurements, one for length and one for weight. We have been doing this for 24 months; thus, we have 24 data points. The data are plotted on a scatter diagram with one axis for length and one for weight.

Scatter Diagram

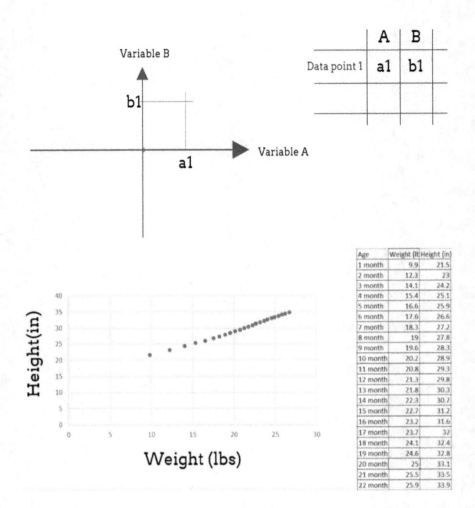

	A	B
Data point 1	a1	b1

Age	Weight (lb)	Height (in)
1 month	9.9	21.5
2 month	12.3	23
3 month	14.1	24.2
4 month	15.4	25.1
5 month	16.6	25.9
6 month	17.6	26.6
7 month	18.3	27.2
8 month	19	27.8
9 month	19.6	28.3
10 month	20.2	28.9
11 month	20.8	29.3
12 month	21.3	29.8
13 month	21.8	30.3
14 month	22.3	30.7
15 month	22.7	31.2
16 month	23.2	31.6
17 month	23.7	32
18 month	24.1	32.4
19 month	24.6	32.8
20 month	25	33.1
21 month	25.5	33.5
22 month	25.9	33.9

There are several ways to show mathematically and statistically how strong a correlation is. It is outside the scope of this section, but you can find it on the internet as correlation statistics or correlation coefficients. The data points can also be interpreted mathematically as an equation. This, too, is outside the scope of this section but can be looked up as regression analysis.

Scatter Diagram

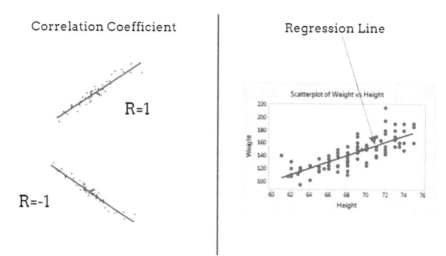

In summary, a scatter diagram is a graphical tool to see whether two variables are related or correlated. Confirming variables as cause and effect is helpful if a positive correlation exists.

2.5. Histogram

A histogram or frequency plot is similar to a stacked bar chart, with each bar representing a range of values, and the height of each bar is the frequency of the data that falls inside that range. Here is the visual explanation of a histogram. A range is a group of values, and each time a data point falls inside the range, it is counted as one or frequency of one; another value within the same range is counted on top of the last one and continues until all data points are plotted.

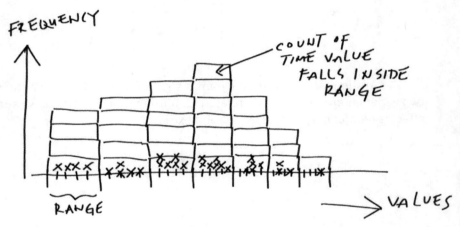

Let's look at an example with data. This set of data has 60 data points. The maximum value is 37, and the minimum value is 10. We want to group the data into eight intervals or 8 bars. Then, the width of each bar is 3.375. We calculate this width: (37-10)/8. The first bar ranges between 10 to 13.375, the second from 13.375 to 16.75, and so on. See how the histogram is done visually.

Histogram

24	24	~~32~~ ⟨37⟩	16	25	~~24~~
14	21	37	16	15	⟨10⟩
18	24	36	18	16	15
27	26	21	30	15	17
17	31	16	21	19	17
32	34	17	16	15	21
31	28	22	14	15	34
27	32	34	15	19	22
21	24	20	14	19	17
27	16	19	14	30	15

$$\frac{(37-10)}{8} = 3.375$$

			16	25	24
			16	15	⟨10⟩
			18	16	15
			30	15	17
			21	19	17
		17	16	15	21
		22	14	15	34
		34	15	19	22
		20	14	19	17
		19	14	30	15

$$\frac{(37-10)}{8} = 3.375$$

PLEASE CONTINUE ON YOUR OWN!

Histogram works best when there are at least 20 data points. Suppose there are fewer than 20 data points; a particular type of histogram is used. It is called a dot plot. Each data point is plotted on the chart as a dot in a dot plot. Unlike a histogram, where data points within an interval are counted as the same, each data value is plotted in a dot plot, and each occurrence is counted and displayed.

Histogram

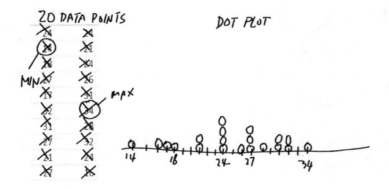

Histogram has several valuable properties. If the shape of the data points or the distribution of data follows a particular type, it can be used to predict the probability of future occurrence. The most common distribution pattern is the normal curve. There are several types of histograms. When the normal curve has two peaks, it is called bimodal. This usually means the process has two main processes, which occur in series or parallel. When the peak is skewed to the left or the right, meaning it is not symmetrical but located to the left or the right of the mid-frequency interval, it can mean the process is not normal.

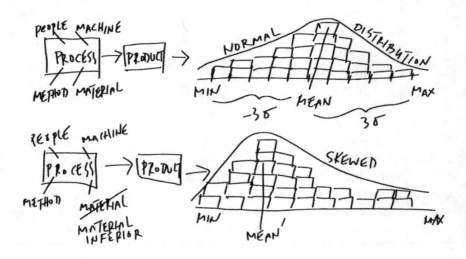

To create a histogram, the max and min values of the observed data must be known. Take the range, the difference between the max and min, and divide it by evenly spaced intervals or the number of bars you want. Too many or too few bars do not show the data pattern well.

A common practice is to take the square root of the data points as the optimum number of bars. For example, if there are 100 data points, the square root is ten, which is the number of intervals. To determine the width of each interval, divide the range of difference between max and min value by 10. The width of each interval is the result of the division.

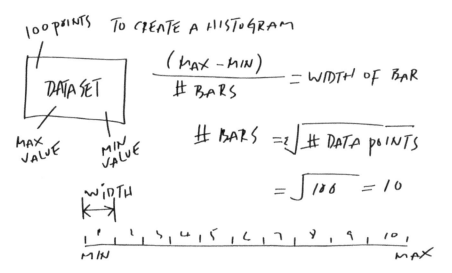

Interpreting the histogram pattern can be done visually, numerically, or statistically. The normal distribution has a bell shape, which is symmetrical around the middle or the mean. The peak of the bell is the point where the frequency of occurrence is the highest. This peak for the normal distribution is also the mean value.

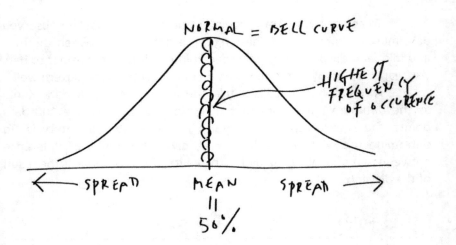

NORMAL = BELL CURVE

HIGHEST
FREQUENCY
OF OCCURENCE

← ——— SPREAD   MEAN   SPREAD ——— →
                  ||
                  50%

2.6. Pareto Diagram

A Pareto chart is a tool to find the vital few causes with the highest effects. These few causes have the most frequent occurrences, such as the highest number of defects or customers with the most complaints. Pareto focuses on where the most significant gains can be made. Thus, it is also a tool to prioritize.

A Pareto chart is a bar chart with three distinct differences: first, the horizontal axis or X axis is a nominal attribute or category data instead of continuous data. Nominal attribute data are categories such as defect names or customer names. Second, the heights of the bars are counts or percents arranged from highest to lowest order from left to right. Third, the cumulative percent line of the bars uses a separate vertical axis or Y axis on the right of the chart with increments from 0% to 100%.

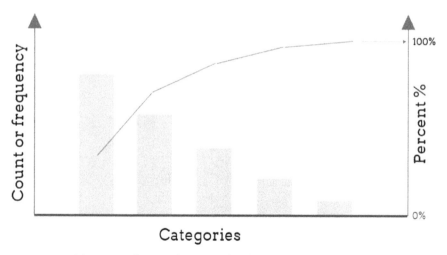

In this example, we have a checksheet of the count of defects sorted by nominal attribute data of customers and defect names. The total defects by defect type and by customer are calculated, and their percentage of the total is shown.

Pareto

	Defect Types							
Customer	A(Scratch)	B(Dent)	C(inop)	D(Leaks)	E(Missing)	F(wrong)	G(broken)	Totals
a	2	1	0	10	2	1		16
b	2	2	0	8	7	2	2	23
c		1	0	7	6		1	21
d	3	0	1	4	5	0	0	23
e	0	1	0	4	9	2	2	18
f	1	3	0	15	5	1		26
Totals	13	8	1	48	34	7	6	117
Percent by defects	11%	7%	1%	41%	29%	6%	5%	
Cumulative percent	11%	18%	19%	60%	89%	95%	100%	

categories

Counts of defects

To draw the Pareto chart, draw a horizontal axis or X-axis and two vertical or Y-axes. The scale of the left Y axis is drawn from the max and min values of the data with equal increments. The scale of the right Y axis is marked from 0% to 100%, with equal increments. List the categories in the order of highest defects to lowest from left to right on the X axis and draw the height of each bar representing the value of each category.

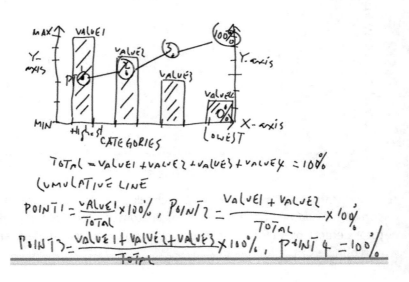

$$TOTAL = VALUE1 + VALUE2 + VALUE3 + VALUEX = 100\%$$

CUMULATIVE LINE

$$POINT1 = \frac{VALUE1}{TOTAL} \times 100\%, \quad POINT2 = \frac{VALUE1 + VALUE2}{TOTAL} \times 100\%$$

$$POINT3 = \frac{VALUE1 + VALUE2 + VALUE3}{TOTAL} \times 100\%, \quad POINT4 = 100\%$$

Pareto

Each bar has a percent cumulative value drawn as a dot in the middle of the bar. The cumulative line connects all the dots. The cumulative line indicates the total effect of the categories as it moves from left to right or from highest to lowest. In this example, to improve the defects by 70%, all top two defects must be eliminated. Therefore, the cumulative line is used to estimate the percent improvement.

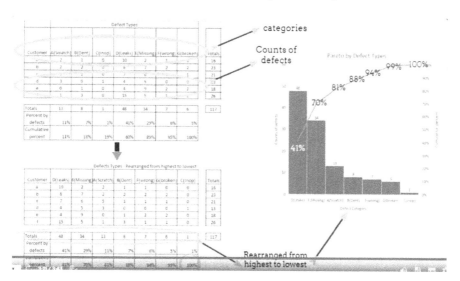

In summary, the Pareto chart is a tool to determine the vital few causes that contribute most to the effects. It is a type of bar chart that has three distinct characteristics:

- The data are nominal attributes or categorical.
- The bars are counts or frequencies of data arranged from highest to lowest and displayed from left to right.
- The cumulative percent line shows the cumulative effect of each bar.

2.7. Control Chart

Control charts are similar to time series and run charts in which the X axis is time data. The Y axis is characteristic to be controlled and can be either an attribute or continuous data type. The two distinct differences between control and other charts are: First, control charts have control limits. Second, the average line or the mean is used as the center line instead of the median, as in the run chart.

- The control limits are typically two lines with values three times the standard deviations from the average line above and below.
- The two control limit lines represent an envelope that contains expected variations over time. If the data distribution is normal, the control limits include 99.7% of all the data points.

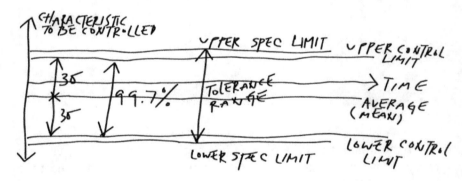

Control limits are not to be confused with specification limits, which sometimes are drawn in the control charts. Control limits should be inside the specification limits. The specification limits are the tolerances specified on the drawing for that particular characteristic.

2.7.1 I-MR chart

In this example, we use an Individual Control chart, or I chart, to measure weekly weight data for 20 weeks to determine the control limits and whether there is a weight loss at the end of 20 weeks.

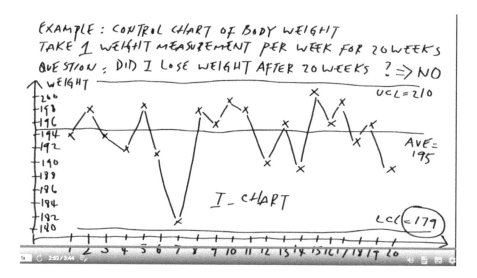

Here are the 20 weekly data points. To make the control chart, the Y axis is the weight, and the X axis is the 20 weeks. The data points are plotted on the chart after each week. At the end of 20 weeks, the average or mean and the control limits are calculated. See the reference section for the calculation. From this control chart, the fluctuation within the two control limits is expected. Statistically, there is no weight loss at the end of 20 weeks because the data is within the control limits. The only time we can claim a weight loss is if the weight is less than the lower control limit.

Control charts are used to monitor the process's variation and detect a special cause if it exists for actions. It is also used to predict the outcome of a process, assuming the process has no special causes. In problem-solving and continuous improvement, control charts are used to monitor the new operating standard procedures after the problem is resolved to prevent reoccurrence or sustain a new condition after it has been improved.

Many control charts depend on the data types collected, such as continuous or attribute. See the diagram below to select the right kind of attribute chart. The readers will practice the simple Individual, moving range control charts in this section. The graph below from Minitab shows different types of control charts.

Control Chart

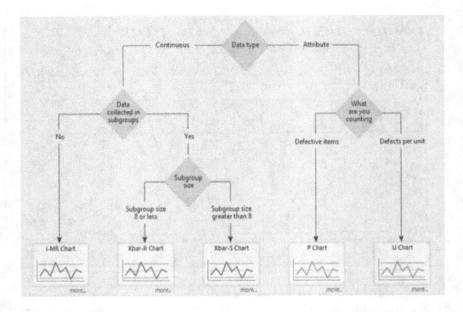

     Big data has limitations with control charts. Because control charts calculate control limits based on a period, big data collected over a long duration may only be helpful for control charts if the user limits the data over a period to calculate control limits.

2.8. Charts (Line, Run, Bar, Pie) and Cautions When Using Them

This section will teach you how to use four standard charts in data analysis for problem-solving and process improvement: line charts, run charts, bar charts, and pie charts. Examples will help you understand the differences between these charts. You can create the appropriate chart for the data collected on the checksheet by the end of this section.

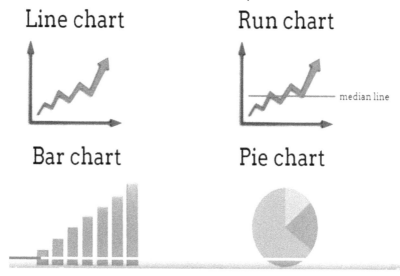

Line charts are time series charts, which are tools for visually displaying data over time to identify trends or patterns. Data are plotted in the order in which they were collected, with regular time intervals between them. As a result, the checksheet for line charts must have accurate time intervals for the data to display correctly. Long-term line charts can exhibit four characteristics: trend, seasonal pattern, cycle, or irregular movement. Trends are the tendency of data to rise or fall over time. Line charts for trends should be used cautiously because the visuals can be deceptive if the coordinates are manipulated. The values in these two charts are identical, but the Y coordinate spacing is different, and the correct chart appears to trend higher than the left chart. The values in these two charts are the same, but the Y coordinate spacing has been changed to make the correct chart appear to fall steeper than the left.

Line chart

— Time series chart

— Four characteristics:

    1. trends,
    2. seasonal patterns,
    3. cycles,
    4. irregular movements

Time

Line chart trends
Tendency of data to rise or fall

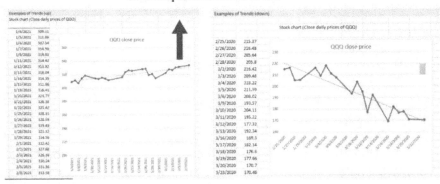

Charts

Seasonal patterns are data shifts that tend to repeat at regular intervals over a specific time frame.

Seasonal patterns
shifts in the data that tend to repeat

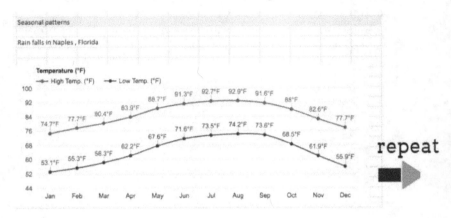

Cycles are data shifts that are not caused by a seasonal pattern; that is, the shifts are not spaced at regular intervals and do not have similar peaks and valleys.

Charts

Cycles

shifts in the data not spaced at regular intervals and values;

Line charts with unusual data points that do not fit into any pattern or trend are examples of irregular movements. Outliers are unusual data points that are sometimes caused by errors in measurement or recording on a checksheet.

Irregular movements

unusual data points that do not fit in any pattern or trends

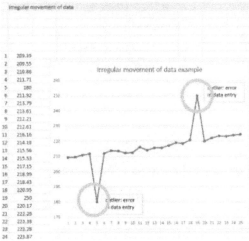

Run charts are visually similar to line charts in that they are time series charts that display the four characteristics of trends and patterns. However, run charts are a more powerful tool in application than line charts because they can provide additional information, such as special causes, if any exist. Special causes are explanations for the behavior of data in trends and patterns.

- Similar to line chart in visual

- More powerful than line chart in application

- Can answer the question: are there special causes in the process?

Finding the causes of the problem or the factors that affect what we want to improve is one of the most essential steps in problem-solving or process improvement because it explains why the data behaves the way it does over time. Causes are classified into three types: common cause, special cause, and root cause. Run charts are simple tools for determining whether or not there are any special causes in the process.

Let's look at an example to see what these three causes mean. Every weekend, a golfer plays golf with his friends. His scores over the last 20 rounds of golf ranged from 100 to 140. The causes of these scores include the types of golf clubs, balls, gloves, shoes, the way he swings the clubs, and put patterns, which have mostly stayed the same in the last twenty years. These are thought to be common causes of his high scores. One day, he decided to break 90 consistently, so he enrolled in golf lessons with a pro. His swing was altered after ten lessons. For the most recent 20 rounds, his scores after the lessons ranged from 80 to 110. The change in his scores results from a special cause, which is the lessons he took. He's still trying to figure out the root cause of the triple bogeys he gets now and then.

Run chart
Example: A golfer

Special causes	Effect
1. Took lessons from a golf pro	
2. Altered the swing pattern	golf scores selected for 20 rounds from oldest to latest after lessons

Round	Score
21	95
22	110
23	90
24	95
25	102
26	95
27	89
28	95
29	93
30	95
31	87
32	80
33	89
34	97
35	103
36	95
37	81
38	92
39	83
40	80

To create a run chart, use the time series checksheet and collect data according to the time intervals on the checksheet. The intervals must not be equal, but they must be chronological, oldest to newest.

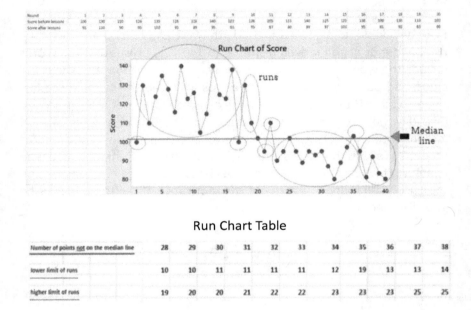

Charts

Draw the median line after collecting data over a period of time. To find the median line, arrange the data in descending order from highest to lowest or ascending order from lowest to highest. The median is the value in the center; draw a line parallel to the X-axis across the median value, and this is the median line.

Round	1	2	3	4	5	6	7	8	9	10	11	12	13	14	15	16	17	18	19	20
Score before lessons	100	130	110	126	135	128	119	140	122	126	105	115	140	125	129	138	130	138	118	102
Score after lessons	90	130	90	85	102	90	89	95	83	95	87	80	99	97	101	95	81	90	63	60

Run Chart Table

Number of points not on the median line	28	29	30	31	32	33	34	35	36	37	38
lower limit of runs	10	10	11	11	11	11	12	13	13	13	14
higher limit of runs	19	20	20	21	22	22	23	23	23	25	25

Another term we must understand to read run charts is the meaning of runs. A run is a series of points that do not cross the median line. To determine whether a special cause exists in the process, consult the run chart table in the reference of this section. If the number of runs is less than the lower limit or greater than the higher limit, a special cause likely exists in the process. If points fall on the median line, do not count these points. Here's an illustration of a golfer.

Charts

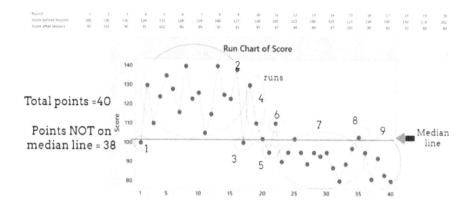

Run Chart of Score

Total points =40

Points NOT on
median line = 38

Median line

The Run chart table is a statistical table with three rows of data: the number of points not on the median line and the lower and upper limits of runs. Look up the total number of points not on the median line first; in this case, are 38 points not on the median line. Then, please compare the actual number of runs; in this case, nine runs are less than the lower limit of 14. We can conclude that the process data has a special cause. The special cause is the lessons the golfer took that caused the change in his scores.

Number of points not on the median line	28	29	30	31	32	33	34	35	36	37	38
lower limit of runs	10	10	11	11	11	11	12	19	13	13	14
higher limit of runs	19	20	20	21	22	22	23	23	23	25	25

Number of points NOT on median line = 38
Actual number of runs = 9
it is fewer than 14

Therefore, Special Cause exists!!!

Bar charts are used to compare data and statistics such as averages, means of characteristics, groups, and categories of things. The height of the bars represents the value of the data or statistics being compared. Bar charts are classified into three types: simple, cluster, and stack.

Charts

A simple bar chart displays the number of unique values for a single variable. The attribute nominal or counts checksheet type is appropriate for a simple bar chart. In this example, we use a simple bar chart to display the defect flaws by categories of paint defects: Peel, scratch, smudge, and others. Peel has the highest defect counts.

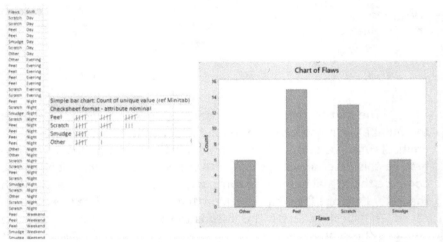

Cluster bar charts display the counts of different levels of each variable. Cluster checksheet are attribute nominal, with columns for the levels of each variable. In this example, we want to know the light output of different glass types and temperatures. Each test is run three times, and the mean value is plotted as the bar charts.

Cluster bar charts

Checksheet Attribute count

Temp	Glass type	Light Output	Mean
100	1	580,568,570	573
100	2	550,530,579	553
100	3	546,575,599	573
125	1	1090,1087,1085,	1087
125	2	1070,1035,1000	1035
125	3	1045,1053,1066	1055
150	1	1392,1380,1386,	1386
150	2	1328,1312,1299	1313
150	3	867,904,889	887

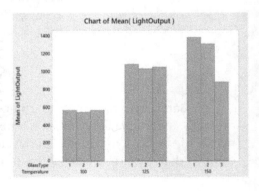

Charts

Stack bars are similar to cluster bars, but instead of having individual bars in a cluster, the bars are stacked. Another example of stack chart is when all the bars are the same height representing 100% and the value inside each bar is the percent of total. When the metrics and values are the same, in this case percentage of population, the segments of the stack bar charts can be compared with other charts. A bar chart can also be used to compare continuous data as long as the units are the same.

Stack bar charts

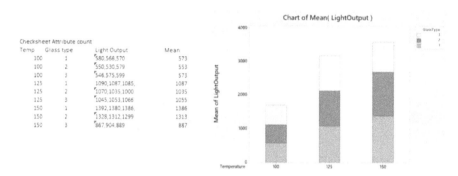

Stack bar chart example

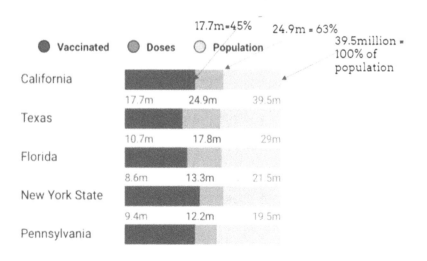

Charts

Pie charts are used to compare percentage or proportional values of variables. A pie is a 360-degree circle that represents 100%. The pie is divided into segments to represent the percentage of the variables' proportion. The attribute percent checksheet is used for pie charts. The checksheet for continuous data can also be used for a pie chart, with additional columns for the proportions of the values in percentages. When interpreting pie charts, consider the various sizes of the slices or segments of the pie to compare the relative sizes of the segments that make up the whole group.

In this example, we use the same data for paint defects and display it in pie chart instead of bar chart. Each category of defects is a percentage of the total defects found during a certain period of time. Peel defects are 38% of total defects.

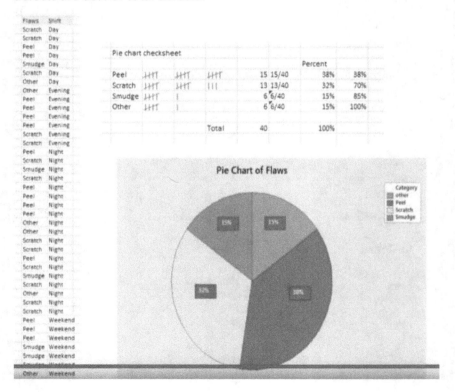

Flaws	Shift
Scratch	Day
Scratch	Day
Peel	Day
Peel	Day
Smudge	Day
Scratch	Day
Other	Day
Other	Evening
Peel	Evening
Peel	Evening
Peel	Evening
Peel	Evening
Scratch	Evening
Scratch	Evening
Peel	Night
Scratch	Night
Smudge	Night
Scratch	Night
Peel	Night
Peel	Night
Peel	Night
Peel	Night
Other	Night
Other	Night
Scratch	Night
Scratch	Night
Peel	Night
Scratch	Night
Smudge	Night
Scratch	Night
Other	Night
Scratch	Night
Scratch	Night
Peel	Weekend
Peel	Weekend
Peel	Weekend
Smudge	Weekend
Smudge	Weekend
Other	Weekend

Pie chart checksheet

						Percent	
Peel	⊞	⊞	⊞	15	15/40	38%	38%
Scratch	⊞	⊞	|||	13	13/40	32%	70%
Smudge	⊞				6	6/40	15%	85%
Other	⊞				6	6/40	15%	100%
Total				40		100%	

Pie Chart of Flaws

Category: other, Peel, Scratch, Smudge

15% | 15% | 32% | 38%

A few cautions when using pie charts. Pie charts should not be compared with other pie charts with different diameters. The segments may appear larger when the diameter is bigger or when the pie is shown in 3D, the segment may be distorted.

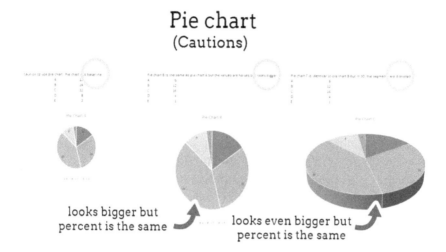

Pie chart
(Cautions)

looks bigger but
percent is the same

looks even bigger but
percent is the same

In summary, charts visualize data. You learned about line charts, run charts, bar charts, and pie charts in this section. Line charts and run charts are time series that show how data changes over time. The bar chart and pie chart are used to compare variables, groups, and categories. Because these graphs can be manipulated to distort the true picture, they should be used with caution.

2.9 Errors to Avoid When Using These Tools

This section will teach you the potential errors and countermeasures when using these tools.

For the histogram, it is easy to make the wrong conclusion that the dispersion or the spread between max and min bars is the same as the population dispersion. Sample data is a subset of the population data, and statistics calculate population parameters. So, avoid making this conclusion without statistical knowledge. The larger the sample size, the closer it is to the population.

The second error for the histogram is to show too few or too many bars. This is due to too much data or not enough data. The rule of thumb is to use this formula: the number of bars is the square root of the data points. For example, if there are 100 data points, the square root is 10, which is the number of bars we should have. The third error is to use a histogram when there are only 20 data points or fewer. When data points are fewer than 20, use data plots instead.

Tools	Errors	Countermeasures	Visuals
Histogram	1) Wrong dispersion conclusion: sample dispersion is the same as population dispersion	Avoid making inferences about the population without statistical knowledge. Increase the size of sample.	POPULATION ⟶ SAMPLE
	2) Frequency bars too few or too many	Use the formula: # of bar is square root of data points. For example, if there are 100 data points, then use 10 bars	OR # bars = √data points
	3) Histogram of a very small sample size (less than 20 data points)	When number of data points fall below 20, use individual data plot instead of histogram.	Fewer than 20

For cause-and-effect diagram, the first error is to constrain its use to the 5M or man, machine, method, materials, and measurement. Cause and effect are a power tool that can be more than 5M. In fact, all ideas should be considered in cause-and-effect diagram and group them in categories for ease of viewing and discussion. There is no rule about the number of bones the fishbone diagram should have. Start a new diagram if there are too many causes. Or if there are not enough ideas, use the internet to find ideas.

The second error is to list only known causes that have affected the problem. Known causes and unknown causes should be considered and what was known before may not be the same as now. Causes that are not relevant will be crossed out.

The third error is to list too many causes or too few causes which makes it looks too busy or too skinny. There is no specific number of causes that must be listed but it must look visually right.

Tools	Errors	Countermeasures	Visuals
Cause and Effect diagram	1) Limited to only 5M (man, machine, method, materials, measurement)	Use Affinity diagram to group causes into categories, not limited to 5M	
	2) List only known causes or causes that are known to affect the problem	Brain storm ideas are listed, if not affect the problem, they will be crossed out	
	3) Too complex with many causes or too few causes	There is no specific number of causes to be listed, if too many, start a new diagram, if too few, use the internet	

For checksheet, the first common error is to use checksheet that is not well designed to meet an objective. Later most data are found useless because it lacks integrity and causes a waste of time and effort. To countermeasure this tendency, ask why the checksheet is used and other pertinent information such as what measurement tool is used, who collects the data, when the sample was made, etc. before the data are collected. Also, it is a good practice to try it out on a few data points before finalizing it.

The second error is checksheet is thought to be used for tally marks only. Tally is only one type of data, checksheet is used for all kinds of data and it is to collect data for analysis. It can be both attribute and continuous. See checksheet section for type of data.

The third error is checklist is confused with checksheet. Checklist is a subset of checksheet, it is a type of checksheet where a list of check items is written down and the data are typical binomial or yes, no, true or false.

Tools	Errors	Countermeasures	Visuals
Checksheet	1) Not well designed for the objectives. Later find most data are useless, waste time and effort	Ask the purpose of checksheet first and trial a few data points	
	2) Only for tally marks	Checksheet is used for tally marks but also for numberic and nominal attribute and ordinal attribute	
	3) Same as checklist	Checklist is usually Yes, No data, while checksheet can include more than Y/N	

For pareto diagram, the first common error is to draw pareto the same as histogram with bars arranged from high to low. The most important line in a pareto is the cumulative percent line and it needs to be drawn with the frequency bars.

The second error is having too many bars with similar heights or magnitude. In this case, group the bars so that 95% of data are displayed in a few bars and the right tail can be grouped into one bar called "Others."

The third error is having too few bars in this case, breaking the data into smaller groups or categories.

Tools	Errors	Countermeasures	Visuals
Pareto	1) Same as histogram but bars are arranged high to low order	Pareto has cummulative perccent line. This is the strength of Pareto	
	2) Too many bars, bars with similar height or magnitudes	Group the bars, especially the right tails into "Others" bar for the last 5% cum line	
	3) Too few bars, looks like two bar charts	Bars should explain contributions of 95% datapoints	

Errors to Avoid When Using These Tools

For graphs in general, the common error is the make the pie chart in 3D. Although it looks more sophisticated with 3D, it is more difficult to compare the segments. Pie chart is used for comparison of the segments or slices in each pie. Use 2D pie chart as a rule of thumb.

The second error is to treat the run chart the same as line chart. A run chart is a statistical chart where special causes can be found as causes of variations over time. Line chart is pure variation and does not have to be time series.

The third error is time series chart is thought to be used for variation study and it cannot be converted into histogram. Line chart data can be converted into histogram when a data over a period of time is frozen, then the data are dropped onto the Y axis to form a dot plot or histogram tilted 90degrees.

Tools	Errors	Countermeasures	Visuals
Graphs	1) Use 3D for interpretation	3D distorts graphs. Pie charts and bar charts should use 2D for segment comparisons	
	2) Run chart is same as Line chart	Run chart is time series chart with statistical analysis. Line chart does not have to be time series	LINE RUN
	3) Data for time series chart cannot be used for histogram	When a period of time is frozen, data within the window can be used for histogram	HISTOGRAM

For control charts, the first error is to confuse control limits as specification limits, they are different. control limits are derived from the process and specification limits are product tolerances.

The second error is to confuse control charts with control plans. Control chart is one of the elements of control plan. Control plans can have many control charts, one for each characteristic to be controlled specified in the control plan.

The third error is to interpret the control chart wrong. Such as special cause only exists when a data point is outside the control limit. Special causes can exist even if all points are within control limits as long as they exhibit run or trends or shifts that show the data are not randomly distributed across the mean.

Tools	Errors	Countermeasures	Visuals
Control Charts	1) Control limits are the same as specification limits	Control limits are derived from process, specification limits are product tolerances	
	2) Control charts are the same as control plans	Control charts is one of elements of control plan	
	3) Special cause exists only when data point is outside control limits	Special cause can exist even all points are within control limits if they exhibit trends, runs	

83

For scatter diagram, the first error is to think that only one pair of data is needed for each point. In fact, scatter diagram works better when a pair of samples data is collected for each variable. This way, variations in the relationship of the two variables can be studied.

The second error is that the two variables are always cause and effect. Variables are not always cause and effect but any two variables that we want to know if there is a relationship between them. For example, variables in the fishbone chart can be studied to see if there is a relationship with the head of the fish.

The third error is to use scatter diagram for prediction of data outside the range. This can be done but only with regression analysis and it includes statistical confidence.

Tools	Errors	Countermeasures	Visuals
Scatter Diagram	1) Only one pair of data for each point	A pair of samples data should be collected to study variations between the two variables	
	2) The two variables are cause and effect	Variables are not always cause and effect variables. A relationship exists does not guarantee cause and effect.	
	3) Can use for prediction of data beyond ranges	Use regression analysis for prediction to include statistical confidence	

2.10 Quiz 2: Test Your Knowledge

Question 1:

Grasping the situation is necessary before diving into the problem because:

○ The problem is not always where it appears to be.

○ To avoid quick judgment which can lead to wrong solution.

○ The symptom may be the same as before but the root cause may be different

○ time and effort can be wasted if attacking the wrong problem

○ All of the above

Question 2:

Is Spaghetti diagram one of the 7 traditional QC tools?

○ Yes

○ No, it is not

Question 3:

Does the fishbone chart have 6 main causes: Man, Machine, Method, Materials, Measurement, Environment. ?

○ Yes, this is traditional accepted practice

○ No, it can have other causes.

Test Your Knowledge

Question 4:

How many data points does histogram diagram require ?

○ **50 data points**

○ **100 data points**

○ **150 data points**

○ **20 data points or more**

Question 5:

What is the tool to use to study relationship between two variables ?

○ **Pareto diagram**

○ **Scatter diagram**

○ **Bar chart**

○ **Histogram**

Question 6:

Does fishbone diagram list only known causes?

○ **Yes**

○ **No**

Test Your Knowledge

Question 7:

Is run chart the same as line chart?

○ **Yes, they are the same**

○ **No, run chart is used to study if special cause exists while line chart is used to study variation**

Question 8:

What are control limits on control charts?

○ **They are limits calculated from process variation to show if process is operating normal or abnormal**

○ **They are the same as specification limits**

○ **They are the same as control plans**

○ **They are the same as max and min lines**

Question 9:

Are two variables plotted on scatter diagram always causes and effect ?

○ **Yes**

○ **No**

○ **Three pairs**

Test Your Knowledge

How many frequency bars are required for histogram?

○ 2

○ 3

○ 4

○ 5 or more

○ It depends on number of data points

Section 3: Seven New Management Tools

3.1 5W 2H

5W and 2H are what, when, who, where, why, how, and how much. This is a powerful tool in the form of questions whose answers are data that need to be collected. Therefore, it is used as a checksheet for problem solving, fact gathering and even for future planning.

5W2H can be applied to past situations where it is used to investigate the truth as in investigative journalism. For present situations, it can be used as a checksheet. In manufacturing, the concept of go and see is called Gemba. For future situations, it can be used as a planning tool.

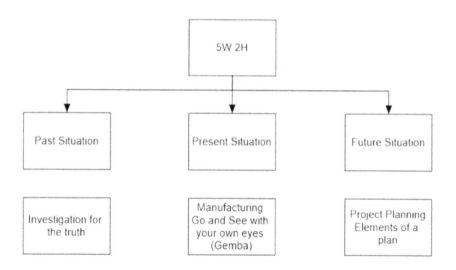

For past situation, since events already happened, 5W2H covers not only a wide area of the situation but it can also go deep into the issue. For example, the use of 5Whys which is one of the 5Ws to search for root cause. In the same line of logic, the 5W 2H can go deep by asking 5Whats, 5Wheres,5Whens, 5whos, 5Hows and 5Howmuchs, each time a question is asked it uses the answer provided previously as the baseline and digs deeper.

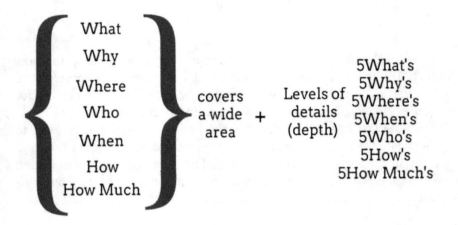

This is an example of using 5W2 for a problem that happened in the past. Please follow the description for explanation

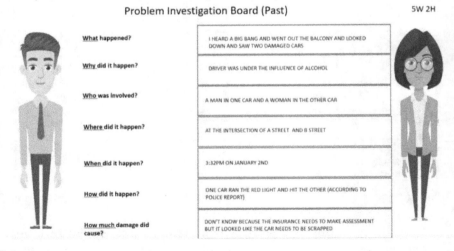

5W2H can also apply to the present situation. In manufacturing, it is encouraged to adopt a principle called Gemba for Go and see with your own eyes since it is happening at this moment. If it is not possible

to go and see, 5W2H can help explain the current situation very well because it covers all the areas of concern.

(Present Situation)

If possible don't ask questions remotely

Go and See and ask questions locally

5W2H

Here is an example of using 5W2H for current situation.

Facts gathering (present)   5W 2H

What is going on?	THE MACHINE IS DOWN
Why is it happening?	THE MOTOR STOPS RUNNING
Who is involved?	THE MAINTENANCE GUY IS LOOKING AT IT RIGHT NOW. THE OPERATOR CALLED THE MAINTENANCE GUY OVER
Where is it happening?	MACHINE A IN THE WORKCELL
When did it start?	10 MINUTES AGO
How can we stop?/start?	WE NEED TO WAIT UNTIL THE ROOT CAUSE IS FOUND, WORST CASE WE HAVE TO REPLACE THE MOTOR
How much does it cost?	EVERY MINUTE DOWNTIME IS $1K, SO FAR IT HAS TAKEN 5 MINUTES

5W2H

For future situations, 5W2H is a great tool to make a plan. Here is a typical plan with all 5W2H included.

5W 2H
(Future Situation)

Purpose: ___WHY___

Items	Timeline	WHEN	WHO Resources	HOW MUCH KPI

Plan / Do / Check

HOW   WHERE

WHAT

man
machine
method
materials

and here is the example of 5W2H when used as questions.

Continuous Improvement Planning Board (Future)   5W 2H

What is the Idea for Improvement?	REDUCE COOKING BREAKFAST TIME TO 5 MINUTES OR LESS
Why do we need to do it?	TO SPEND MORE TIME WITH MY KIDS BEFORE I GO TO WORK
Who is going to do it?	ME
Where is it to be done?	IN THE KITCHEN OF MY APARTMENT
When is it to be done?	AFTER I COMPLETE MY COURSE ON UDEMY
How is it to be done?	USE SPAGHETTI CHART AND FLOW DIAGRAM TO STUDY WASTE OF MOVEMENT AND REDUCE OR ELIMINATE IT
How much do we gain?	$19.99 TO TAKE THE COURSE AND THE GAIN DEPENDS ON HOW MUCH

To deep dive to obtain detailed data, it is necessary to ask 5 questions for each of the 5W2H. Each time, the question uses the previous answer as springboard into the next. Here is an example of 5Whats using pareto diagram. The first What is the highest bar on the pareto. The second what is breaking up the highest bar into a second pareto and the highest bar on the second pareto is the second What. Repeat this process to find the third what which is breaking up the highest bar on the second pareto diagram and make a third pareto, and the highest bar on this third pareto is the third what....

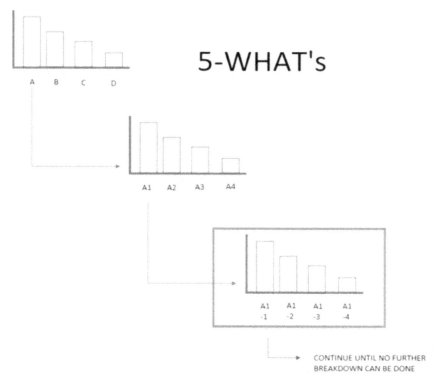

5-WHAT's

93

5W2H

and here are examples 5 Hows,

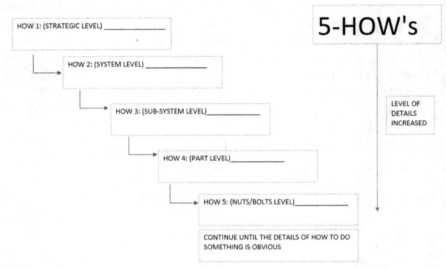

5 Whys

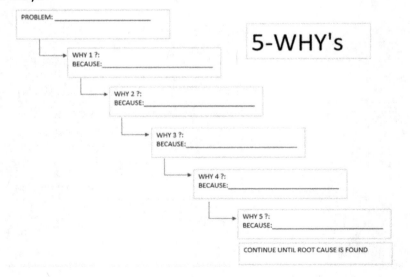

5W2H

5 Where's

5 Whos

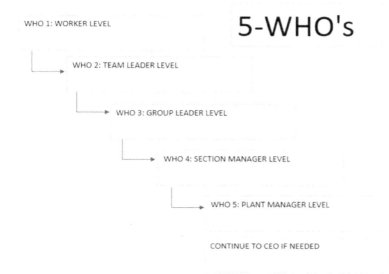

3.2 Matrix Diagram- Cause and Effect Matrix

Cause and effect matrix is similar to cause-and-effect diagram, but the distinct differences are the Cause-and-Effect matrix can have many effects whereas Cause and Effect diagram or fishbone has one effect. The Cause-and-Effect diagram has the shape of a fish whereas the Cause-and-Effect matrix is a matrix with rows and columns.

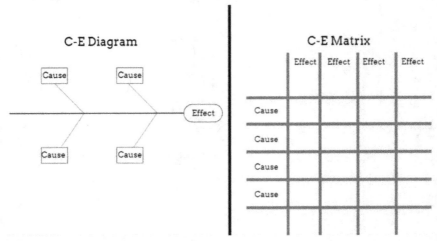

CE matrix connects output variables or effects with input variables or causes with rows and columns. Where columns and rows intersect, the relationships or correlation is identified. Unlike CE diagram where the relationship is assumed linear, CE matrix's relationships can be linear, or nonlinear. The other difference with the CE matrix is that it also has priority ratings or weight factors assigned to the effects.

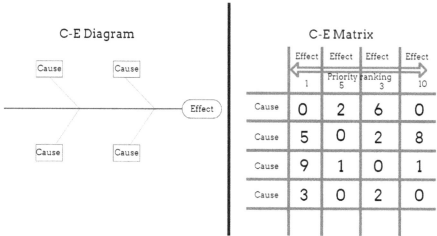

To create a CE matrix, start with output variables at the top of the matrix, these are the effects and input variables at the left-hand side of the matrix, these are the causes. Decide a correlation ranking system, usually 0 to 10, denoting from none to high. A zero or no correlation means the input does not affect the output, a high correlation means the input affects the output strongly. At the intersection of each row and column, provide this correlation number. If there are many output variables and they have different priorities or different importance, give a priority number to each output variable, usually also from 1 to 10, denoting low priority to high priority.

	Effect	Effect	Effect	Effect	
		Priority ranking			Priority of Effect:
	1	5	3	10	1: Low 10: High
Cause1	0	2	6	0	Cause 1: 1x0 + 5x2 + 3x6 +10x0 = 28
Cause2	5	0	2	8	Cause 2: 1x5 + 5x0 + 3x2 +10x8 = 91
Cause3	9	1	0	1	Cause 3: 1x9 + 5x1 + 3x0 +10x1 = 24
Cause4	3	0	2	0	Cause 4: 1x3 + 5x0 + 3x2 +10x0 = 9

Once the correlation numbers are given to each input variable, calculate the results of each input variable across all output variables by multiplying each correlation number with the priority number and total up this number for all the columns. In this example, cause 1 has 28 total points, cause 2 has 91 points, cause 3 has 24 and cause 4 has 9 points.

This result of each input variable is compared with other input variables to show the relative importance of the causes. The cause with the highest multiplication of correlation and priority is the most important cause for investigation, in this case cause 2 is highest with 91 points. This cause is first to be investigated and countermeasures put in place.

In Summary, Cause and Effect matrix is an expanded version of Cause-and-effect diagram where multiple effects are analyzed at the same time for each cause. The relationship between cause and effect is modified by the correlation number, usually from 0 to 10. O is the same as an X in the Fishbone diagram. The effects also have priority number assigned to each one. The total points calculated are ranked to prioritize the cause to be investigated. In the next section, we will show how these variables are prioritized using Pareto principles.

3.3 Affinity Diagram

Affinity diagram is tool to organize data, facts, information, opinions into groups of similar topics or themes. There are usually two approaches to organize big data. Top down and bottom up. Top-down approach uses a predetermined categories or themes and use those to generate ideas such as Man Machine Method Material. Most problem solving uses top down where ideas are generated from a fixed categories to address root cause of a problem. Tools such as Fish bone, 5 Whys, Failure Tree use a top-down approach. Bottom-up approach uses ideas already generated by brainstorming and group them to determine the categories that fit a group of ideas. Affinity diagram uses this approach.

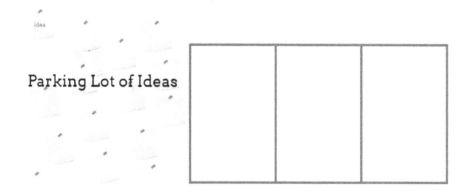

Affinity diagram is tool to organize data, facts, information, opinions into groups of similar topics or themes under headers

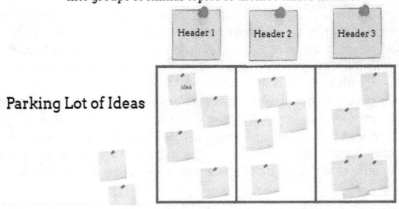

Parking Lot of Ideas

TOP DOWN APPROACH

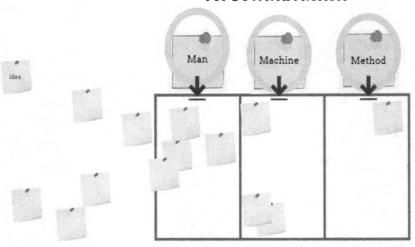

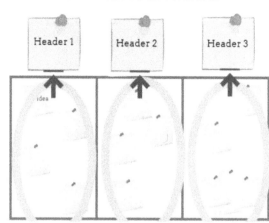

Parking Lot of Ideas

BOTTOM UP APPROACH

Header 1   Header 2   Header 3

Affinity diagram has only two main components: ideas and idea headers. Here is an example of a completed affinity diagram. To generate this diagram, the overall theme or overall header is listed: Creating an online education business during retirement. Then a brainstorming session is done to generate ideas: these are ideas that came up and were captured on sticky notes. Once ideas are generated, they are organized into six headers as shown.

Affinity Diagram

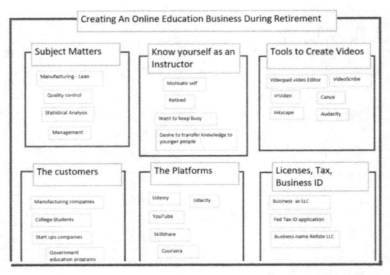

Here is another example of using affinity diagram to reduce the time to cook a breakfast in less than 5 minutes. See this example in the spaghetti chart section.

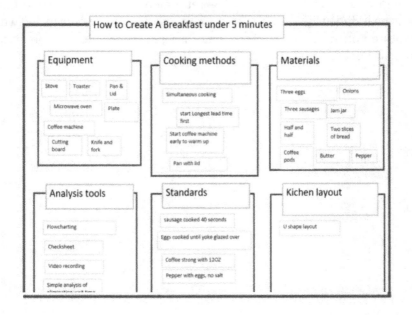

What are the benefits of affinity diagram?. Affinity helps bring chaos into order. When many minds have many ideas come together, affinity diagram can bring ideas to form consensus. A person with many unorganized ideas is restless and worried, affinity diagram brings peace and order. This is important in the planning stage before any actions are taken.

3.4 Relations Diagram

The traditional cause and effect diagram is structured to find specific causes that affect a particular effect. On the other hand, the relations diagram is free thinking technique, and the scope is broad in finding many causes and many effects. Even though both require brainstorming to come up with ideas, relations diagram is used for more complex situations with many scattered issues where cause and effect cannot be established easily.

Traditional CE diagram   Relations Diagram

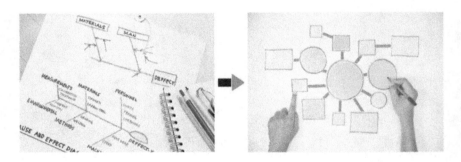

With the advent of the internet, ideas are abundant on the web, and the relations diagram can establish relationships between these ideas with ideas from own experience to form a coherent picture of the many main causes and effects that are helpful to gain insights about the situation.

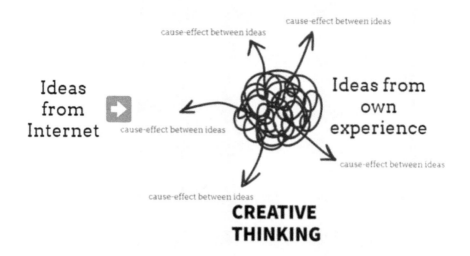

The relations diagram begins with a situation in the center of the page. Free thinking will generate relevant ideas, issues, solutions, activities, and strategies related to the situation that are dispersed throughout the page. When a cause-and-effect relationship between two elements is recognized, an arrow is drawn with the arrow pointing to the effect.

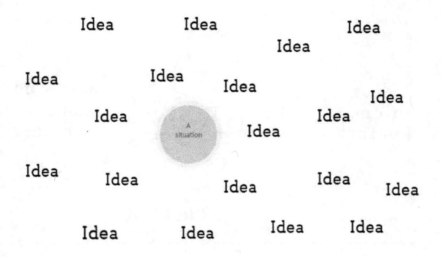

This is an example of a complete relations diagram.

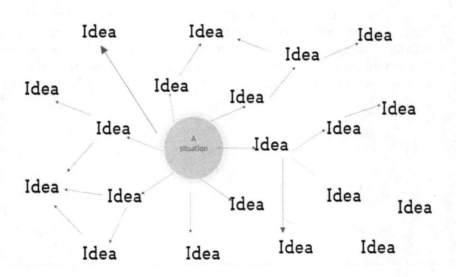

This is how it was constructed step by step. The situation is a question about what constitutes a good team leader in a lean organization. This is written in the page's center. Then, on the periphery of the question, ideas are written down after reflecting on the roles of a team leader from experience and what they actually do. Here are all the ideas associated with a model team leader.

What is a model Team Leader like?

Welcome everyone on the team when they join

Quickly react to Andon calls for help

Be at work early to check the readiness of team before shift starts

Avoid part shortages by alerting Production Control

Helps other teams in the group

Assure work environment is safe

Continuously improve standardized work for team members

Thank the team when they go beyond the call of duty

Check the line for built-in quality

Set a good example for team members

Say, " I can, my team can"

Listen to team members for inputs. Be a good listener

Be genuinely happy to see members come to work

Relations Diagram

Sub for team member
when they have to leave
work early

Perform 5S audit
of the work area

Conduct training
for new member

Review SQDCM
board daily

Conduct 5 minute
pre-shift meeting
to communicate information

Perform Team Leader
standard work

An arrow is drawn between two connecting ideas whenever a cause-and-effect relationship is recognized. This process was repeated until all ideas were reviewed.

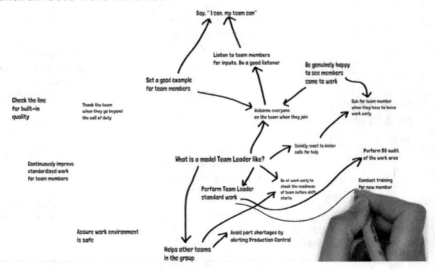

Relations Diagram

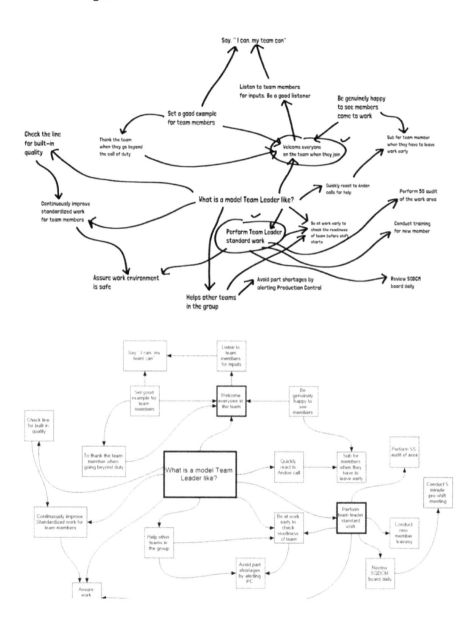

Examine the elements on the map that have the most arrows pointing to or going out after you've completed the map. These are critical elements that have an impact on the situation. The element with the most arrows pointing to it is supposed to be the primary effect or outcome. The element with the most arrows pointing out is the primary cause or driver influencing the situation. In many cases, cause and effect elements do not conform to this rule and it should not be forced to follow as long as the mind is grasping the situation well when it has a good understanding of these key elements.

Returning to the example, the two items that have the most arrows pointing to and going out are: welcoming everyone on the team and performing team leader standard work. These are the two primary activities that a model team leader performs.

Cause and effect for advanced tools such as relations diagram does not conform clearly to the rule because what is the effect can be a cause also. For example, in cascading a business goal as in business deployment, top level goal is the lower-level mean, and so on.

3.5 Systematic Diagrams- Tree Diagram

A tree diagram is a systematic thinking technique used to delve deeper into a situation in order to gain the most detailed insights. This technique aids the mind's transition from generalities to specifics. It is used to accomplish a difficult goal that necessitates the cooperation of everyone in the organization. It can also be used to divide a large problem into smaller ones in order to solve them.

It is an analysis technique as opposed to a synthesis technique, or top down as opposed to bottom up. Analysis breaks things down into smaller parts, whereas synthesis assembles smaller parts into a complete part.

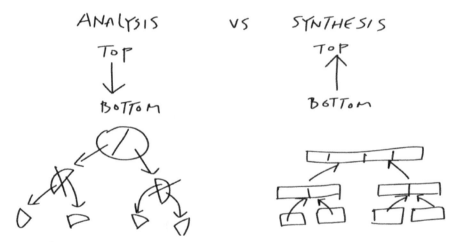

The tree diagram differs from the relations diagram in that the tree diagram has a hierarchy while the relations diagram does not. The tree diagram resembles an organization chart or a fish bone diagram, but there is no brainstorming for the tree and all of the causes along the same branch have a parent-child relationship or are related to one another.

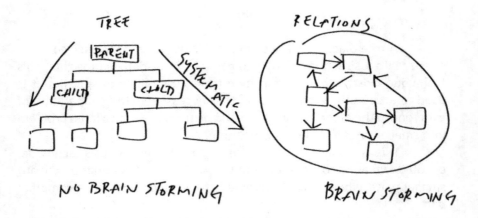

This is an example of a tree diagram. We call this the What - Why tree diagram. The situation or top issue is placed on one side as a what. The first level causes are linked to the issue; these are the whys. To get to the next level we ask why again. For example, to get the first level causes, we ask Why problem happened as one branch, why problem was not detected, this is the second branch, why the system failed, this is the third branch. This is what we call the 3-legged 5 whys approach used in automobile industry. Then each branch is drilled deeper by asking 5 whys as in 5 whys technique.

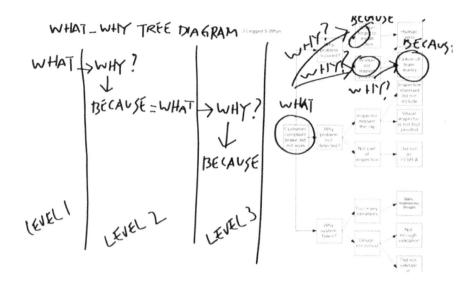

This is another example of a tree diagram; we call it the What - How tree diagram. The situation is a difficult objective, a goal set by the CEO to improve customer satisfaction. This goal is drilled down into the organization by asking How to achieve this objective to each department heads. The first level shows each department head how to improve the customer satisfaction in their functional department, then the lines continue within each department to the lowest level in each departmental organization. This technique is used in Business plan deployment of company goals and objectives.

WHAT-HOW TREE DIAGRAM

WHAT→How
↓
   WHAT→How
   ↓
      WHAT→How

LEVEL1 LEVEL 2 LEVEL 3 LEVEL 4

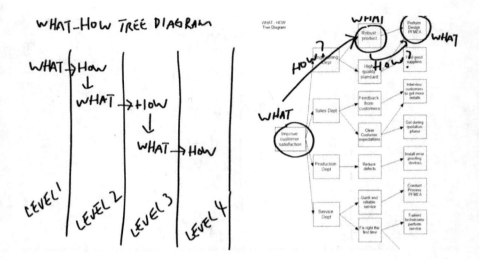

3.6 Arrow Diagram (Activity Network Diagram)

Arrow diagram or activity network diagram manages tasks in a project graphically where the relationships and orders between tasks must be maintained so that problems with scheduling, resources are addressed, and solutions provided. The arrow diagram calculates the "Critical Path" of a project. The critical path is the path that activities follow where any change to an activity on this path will affect the entire project timing. Either delaying it if an activity is delayed or shortening it if an activity is shortened.

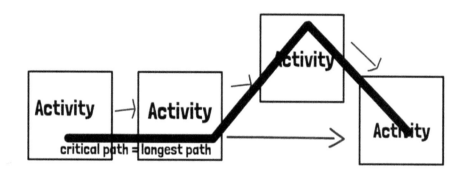

In this example, there are 7 tasks divided into three resources, or three persons. The first person does tasks 1 and 2, the second person does tasks 3 to 6, third person task 7. The critical path is the longest time from start to end which is the path that goes from start to task 1 to 2 to 6 to end calculated to be 20 minutes. task 2 must be completed before task 6 and task 7 must be completed before task 5. Using this arrow diagram, one can see the use of resources is not efficient because there is waste of idle time for all three resources. The challenge is to better use resources without affecting critical path. One solution is to move task 6 to resource #1, task 7 to resource #2. The resource needed now is only two instead of three. This is one application of arrow diagram.

Arrow Diagram

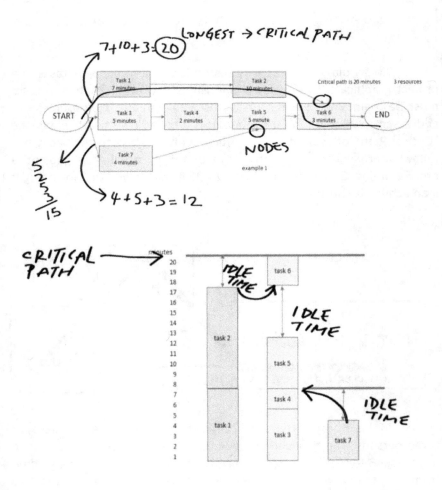

LONGEST → CRITICAL PATH

7+10+3=(20)

Task 1
7 minutes

Task 2
10 minutes

Critical path is 20 minutes   3 resources

START

Task 3
5 minutes

Task 4
2 minutes

Task 5
5 minute

Task 6
3 minutes

END

Task 7
4 minutes

NODES

example 1

5
2
3
/15

4+5+3 = 12

CRITICAL ⟶ minutes
PATH

20
19   IDLE   task 6
18   TIME
17
16   IDLE
15   TIME
14
13   task 2
12
11
10   task 5
9
8
7   task 4
6
5
4   task 1
3   task 3
2   task 7
1

IDLE
TIME

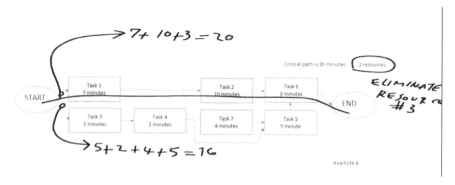

$$7 + 10 + 3 = 20$$

Critical path is 20 minutes   2 resources

| Task 1 7 minutes | Task 2 10 minutes | Task 6 3 minutes |
| Task 3 5 minutes | Task 4 2 minutes | Task 7 4 minutes | Task 5 5 minute |

START   END

ELIMINATE RESOUR #3

$$5 + 2 + 4 + 5 = 16$$

example 4

NO IDLE FOR RESOURCE #1

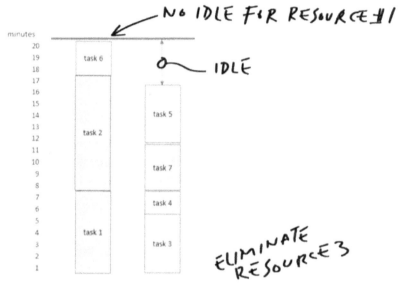

IDLE

ELIMINATE RESOURCE 3

Move tasks without affecting the critical path, resources are more efficient

Arrow diagram is used to control schedules and for estimating the best way to complete the entire project when there are many activities involved and a balance of timing, risks and resources are demanded. Overall timing can be reduced by reducing time of activities on the critical path. Here is an example of reducing the time of task 2 from 10 minutes to 4 minutes, the critical path is changed. It is now 15 minutes from start to end and it travels along different activities. Looking at this arrow diagram, one sees opportunities to add more tasks to resource #1 and resource #3 without affecting the critical path as shown here.

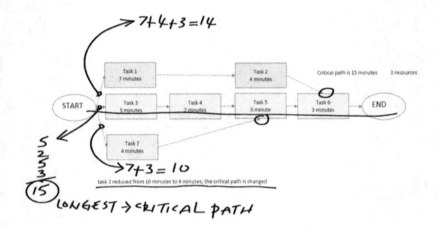

To construct an arrow diagram, start with a beginning, usually an oval with the word starts inside. This is similar to process flow diagram, but each activity has a start time and an end time or the duration time, a resource information, the order of occurrence for each activity, in other words, some activities are pre-requisite to others. Write each activity inside a rectangle, indicate the time it takes to complete. Then, link up all these activities by arrows in the sequence of occurring, either in series of one another or in parallel of one another. Then determine the critical path. It is the path that has the longest total time. Determine the resources or number of people needed to perform these activities. The two main Key process indicators for arrow diagram are the critical path time and resources including people and machines.

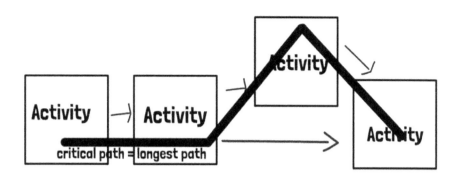

Here is an example where tasks are added to the projects without changing the critical path to make better use of resources. If task #8 is added to resource 3 and task # 9 is added to resource 1, the critical path remains the same.

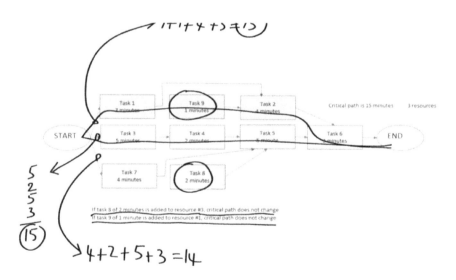

3.7 Process Decision Program Chart (PDPC)

The process decision program chart, or PDPC, determines the process to be used and systematically identifies what could go wrong so that desired results could be achieved. PDPC deals with risks and countermeasures for each element of the process. What is risk? a future uncertainty of not meeting an objective due to not having enough information, excessive variations in the process, unforeseen issues, or unmanaged changes.

Countermeasures of risks include risk avoidance, risk reduction, and contingency plan. Risk avoidance is avoiding taking the actions involving identified risks, including taking alternatives or in worst case abandoning the plan. Risk reduction is taking actions to reduce risk such as confirming assumptions, reducing variations in the process, and making procedures to review changes. Contingency plans include making plans to confront risks if they do occur, this includes additional actions in case risks become reality.

To construct a PDPC, start with a process with actions to meet an objective. For each action element in the process, identify what could go wrong, these are risks being addressed. Address each risk with countermeasures.

Objective: _

Process Elements	**Potential problems or Risks**	**Countermeasures**

The most common PDPC in manufacturing is the Process Failure Mode and Effect Analysis chart or PFMEA. PFMEA is a risk evaluation and reduction plan for a process. Risk is quantified into a numeric value called RPN or Risk priority number. It is a multiplier of three factors: Severity,

Occurrence and Detection. Each factor has a 1 to 10 scale from lowest to highest. A RPN of 1 is the lowest possible risk, a RPN of 1000 is the highest possible risk. Here is an example of a PFMEA template.

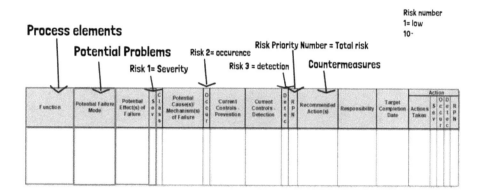

Let's look at an example of PDPC of changing a flat tire using PFMEA.

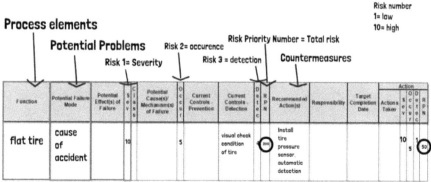

No change to severity risk, remains at 10
No change to occurence risk, remains at 5
Change to detection risk, lowered from 4 to 1

In this example, the process element is flat tire, the potential problem caused by flat tire is accident during driving. The first risk is the severity of failure and we give it a 10 which is the highest possible risk, the second risk is occurrence risk, how likely does flat tire happen while driving, here we estimate risk of 5 which is middle of the scale, the third risk is detection, how likely can we detect if a flat tire does occur before we drive off the car, we give it a 4 because we can check the tires by visually looking at them. There is no guarantee if the flat tire occurs during driving. The RPN is 200 which is a multiplier of 10,5 and 4. This RPN of 200 is deemed excessive so countermeasures must be taken to reduce risks. We decided to install a tire pressure sensor so if the flat tire occurs at any time, a light will come on in the dashboard. So, detection risk is reduced from 4 to 1. The other two risks remain the same. The new RPN is 50 which is the multiplier of 10,5 and 1.

3.8 Matrix Data Analysis

Matrix data analysis arranges data in a matrix form for ease of visualization and understanding. It is used when a set of variables behaving similarly within two identified characteristics are plotted on an X-Y chart. This makes it easy to see how the variables are related to the two characteristics and to one another.

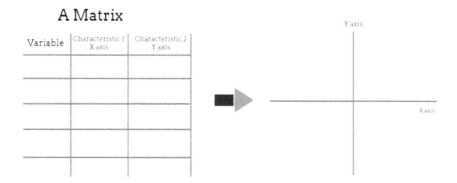

Here is an example of a Matrix Data Analysis Plot. In this example, the variables are names of persons and the department the person is in. The two characteristics are responses of the person to the questions: how concerned are you for production and how concerned are you for quality? Using the ranking of 1 to 10, 1 being not concerned at all and 10 very concerned. To construct this matrix data analysis plot, start with a checksheet with column for variables, characteristic 1, and for characteristic 2. Once the data is collected, they are plotted on an X-Y graph. This is the graph of an example. From the graph we see three clusters of similarities, one of production personnel who have higher concern for production than for quality, another cluster of quality personnel who has higher concern for quality than production and a single person cluster who neither concerns for production nor quality. Comparing this graph with the targeted graph in mind which has personnel in the quadrant where concern for production and quality is high, the company can make decisions on training of existing employees and for hiring new employees in the future.

Matrix Data Analysis

Q1: How concern are you for production? (1:low, 10: high)

Q2: How concern are you for quality?

Variables	Characteristic 1 = Concern for Production	Characteristic 2 = Concern for Quality
John (Production manager)	8	3
Joe (Quality manager)	2	10
Mike (Quality Engineer)	3	9
Bob (Production supervisor)	7	4
Andy (Team leader Producti	9	4
Jaime (Production superviso	9	3
Victor (QC supervisor)	6	9
Jose (Foreman Production)	9	1
Tony (QC inspector)	1	10
Michelle (QCE manager)	8	9
Sam (warehouse)	3	3

Q1: How concern are you for production? (1:low, 10: high)

Q2: How concern are you for quality?

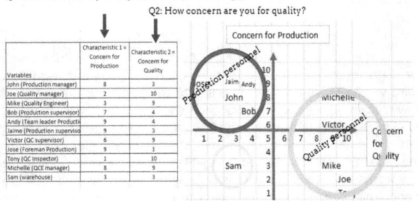

124

Matrix Data Analysis

Target Graph

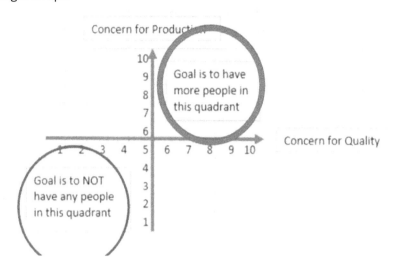

Concern for Product

Goal is to have
more people in
this quadrant

Concern for Quality

Goal is to NOT
have any people
in this quadrant

Data can also be attribute nominal or ordinal. In this example, we survey four products A, B, C, D to get customers' opinions about some features. A survey was conducted, and customers were asked two identical questions about each product. One question about their positive experience of the product, for example: How would you feel if the product feature A performed as you expected? Another question about their negative experience of the product, for example: How would you feel if the product feature A did not perform as you expected. The customer has four answer choices: I like it, it is normal, I don't care about it, I don't like it. Here is an example of the checksheet. The response on the checksheet is compared to a model response to classify the products into three categories: Delighters, satisfiers or dissatisfiers. This method is called the Kano model. Companies strive to design products with new features to move into the delighters category, where customers are excited because they experience unexpected features and tend to complain less about problems. In this example, product B meets the classification of "Delighters" and is the best product.

Survey four products: A,B,C,D
Customers are asked two identical questions:

Q1: How would you feel if the product __ performed as you expected

Q2: How would you feel if the product ___ did not perform as you expected?

Customers have 4 answer choices: I like it,
It is normal,
I don't care about it,
I don't like it.

Products Survey Questions (1 Positive question and 1 Negative question)	Answers (Like) (Normal) (Don't care) (Don't like)	Type of customers
Product A How would you feel if the product feature A performed as you expected?	Normal	Satisfiers
Product A How would you feel if the product feature A did not perform as you expected?	Don't like	Satisfiers
Product B How would you feel if the product feature B performed as you expected?	Like	Delighters
Product B How would you feel if the product feature B did not perform as you expected?	Normal	Delighters
Product C How would you feel if the product feature C performed as you expected?	Don't care	Dissatisfiers
Product C How would you feel if the product feature C did not perform as you expected?	Don't like	Dissatisfiers

Model

		Answers to NEGATIVE questions			
		Like	Normal	Don't care	Don't like
Answers to POSITIVE questions	Like		delighter	delighter	satisfier
	Normal				dissatisfier
	Don't care				dissatisfier
	Don't like				

Products Survey Questions (1 Positive question and 1 Negative question)	Answers (Like) (Normal) (Don't care) (Don't like)	Type of customers
Product A How would you feel if the product feature A performed as you expected?	Normal	Satisfiers
Product A How would you feel if the product feature A did not perform as you expected?	Don't like	Satisfiers
Product B How would you feel if the product feature B performed as you expected?	Like	Delighters
Product B How would you feel if the product feature B did not perform as you expected?	Normal	Delighters
Product C How would you feel if the product feature C performed as you expected?	Don't care	Dissatisfiers
Product C How would you feel if the product feature C did not perform as you expected?	Don't like	Dissatisfiers

Kano
Model

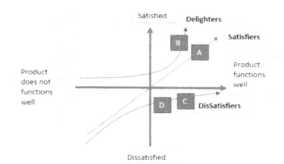

<u>Conclusion:</u>

Product B is
the best.
It is a
"Delighter"

Delighers: Customers excited with new product because there unexpected features that wow them,they are more tolerant with problems

Satifiers: This is standard customer response. Customers are happy about product, when it performs as expected, if not they are unhappy.

Dissatisfiers: Customers are not excited about the product, demand basic

In summary, Matrix data analysis arranges data in matrix forms and plots them on XY coordinates of characteristics being studied. This makes it easy to see how the variables are related to the two characteristics and to one another.

3.9 Quiz 3: Test Your Knowledge

Question 1:

Is Cause and Effect matrix similar to Cause and Effect diagram?

○ **Yes because they study causes and effects**

○ **No, because one is matrix and the other is a diagram**

○ **No, because cause and effect matrix can study many effects and many causes at the same time, while cause and effect diagram studies only one effect and many causes**

Question 2:

How many components does Affinity diagram have ?

○ **One, the Headers**

○ **Two, the Headers and the Ideas**

○ **Three, the Headers, Ideas and Analysis**

Question 3:

What tool is used to study complex relationships between many variables initially?

○ **Systematic diagram**

○ **Affinity diagram**

○ **Relations diagram**

○ **Matrix diagram**

○ **Arrow diagram**

Test Your Knowledge

Question 4:

What are the main indicators for arrow diagram?

○ **Critical path and resources**

○ **Resources and number of activities**

○ **Critical path**

Question 5:

What tool is used to assess risks ?

○ **Relations diagram**

○ **Affinity diagram**

○ **Process Decision Program Chart (PDPC)**

○ **Matrix data analysis**

Question 6:

What is the difference between errors and lies ?

○ **Errors are interpreting charts wrongly because lack of knowledge, Lies are interpreting charts wrongly because the person wants to deceive the readers of the charts.**

○ **Errors are poor judgments, lies are withholding correct judgments**

○ **Errors are when the mind sees reality not correctly, lies are when the mind sees reality correctly but the person says something different**

Test Your Knowledge

Question 7:

Is Tree diagram the same as 5 Why's?

○ **Yes, both are systematic diagrams**

○ **No, Tree diagram is systematic diagram, 5 Why's is root cause analysis**

○ **No, Tree diagram is horizontal, 5Why's is vertical**

Section 4: Tools Synthesis Introduction

Tool synthesis is a technique applying the proper set of tools in the correct sequence to a particular situation to achieve the objectives or solutions. The tool synthesis section is essential for learning how to maximize the power of these tools. The universal principle is PDCA or the Plan Do Check Act.

Although most tools can be used independently, they work best when used in a logical order. In continuous improvement, tools are typically used in the following order: 5W2H, flowchart, checksheet, graphs, Pareto, fishbone, matrix diagram, and control charts. We will review the details of this order, and you will see why using tools sequentially in this order will result in long-term improvement.

In this section, you will learn three methods of selecting tools for your situations. The first method is called the problem-solving or continuous improvement method. Here is the diagram, which we will return to and go over in detail. The second method is called descriptive to preventive. The third method is the stratification of tools based on types of data. There are examples of each method to help you understand the logic behind each one.

Sequence of tools used in a continuous improvement project.

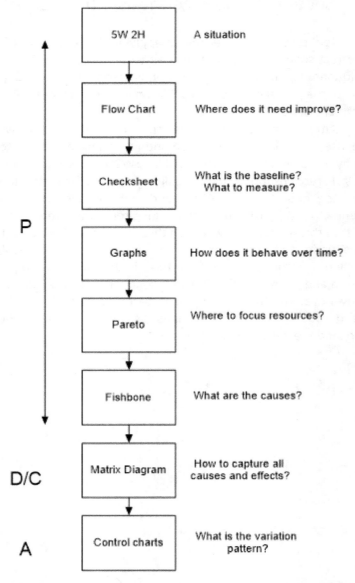

Looking at this process from the Six Sigma perspective of DMAIC (Define, Measure, Analyze, Improve, and Control), we start with a situation or often a problem to be solved. The tool to break down the situation or problem is 5W2H, What, Why, Where, When, Who, How, and How much.

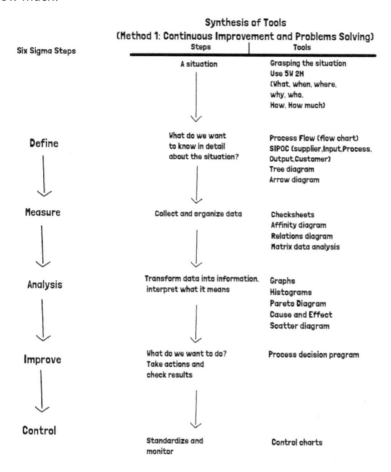

Next, what do we want to know about the situation or problem in detail? This is the equivalent step in Six Sigma problem solving as Define. We set the objective and define the scope and goal. Tools used include process flow, SIPOC, tree diagram, or arrow diagram.

The third step is to collect and organize data. This is equivalent to Measure in 6- sigma. Tools used include checksheet, affinity diagram, relations diagram, and matrix data analysis.

The fourth step is transforming data into information and interpreting what it means. The power of tools comes into play; as long as data remains data and not useful information, tools are useless. The power of tools is to convert data into something we can understand and help us make decisions. Here, graphs, line graphs, bar graphs, pie charts, histograms, Pareto diagrams, cause and effect diagrams, or fishbone and scatter diagrams are helpful for the conversion. This step is equivalent to the Analysis phase of DMAIC.

The fifth step is what we want to do with the situation, or the problem presented to us, what actions we should take, and the risk involved. Here, the PDPC or process decision program chart can be used. This step is equivalent to Improve in DMAIC. Other tools can also be used, but we mention the main one here.

Finally, the sixth step is to standardize and monitor. This is to lock in the gain we have achieved so far. The problem is solved, and the situation is meeting its objectives. If not, returning to the previous steps is the standard course of action before standardization.

4.1 Synthesis Method 1: Continuous Improvement and Problem Solving

In this section, we will walk through an example to show the application of tool synthesis in a continuous improvement situation. Let's review the process of tool synthesis for this method. first we grasp the situation by using the 5W2H tool, next we want to define what we want to know in detail, then we want to organize data by collecting relevant data and organize them in easy-to-understand format. we then transform the data into information and interpret what it means, this is called analysis phase, then we want to take action to improve the situation or solve the problem, and finally we want to standardize and monitor the improved situation, so we don't slip backward.

Situation	What do we want to know in detail?	Collect and organize data	Transform data, obtain insight	Take action and check result?	Standardize and monitor
Grasping the situation, 5W 2H	Process flow chart SIPOC Tree diagram Arrow diagram	Checksheet Affinity diagram Relations diagram Matrix data analysis Graphs	Graphs Histograms Pareto diagram Cause and effect Scatter diagram	Process decision diagram Matrix diagram	Control chart

Six Sigma →	Define	Measure	Analysis	Improve	Control

Here is the matrix diagram explaining the example we will show here. On the left column is the process we just described with details of the example. The situation is a college student having some financial problems. He feels that the expenses are out of control and wants to do something about it. Here will use the 5W2H tool.

Tools Synthesis Method 1

Example 1: A college student wants to control costs					
Situation	What do we want to know in detail?	Collect and organize data	Transform data, obtain insight	Take action and check result?	Standardize and monitor
A college student wants to control costs because he feels his personal expenses are out of control	The details of the costs in the last 12 months and what are the major cost items	Checksheet to collect data of costs and classify them in categories, draw line chart over the last 12 months	What are the top cost items, and why does he feel costs are out of control? Is it true? What are the reasons for major expenses?	Wants to know if he wants to reduce the costs by 20% over the next 12 months. What does he have to do?	He wants to establish a cost control process to alert when the cost is spiraling out of control and to take action before it does.
5W 2H	Process flow chart	Checksheet Affinity diagram Graphs	Graphs Pareto diagram Cause and effect	Process decision diagram Matrix diagram	Control chart

Next he wants to know the details of the costs in the last 12 months and what are the major cost items. For this example, we will use a process map.

Then to organize data, he first wants to collect data by using a checksheet and classify them in categories, draw a line chart over the last 12 months. The tools he wants to use are checksheet, graph, an affinity diagram.

Then he wants to transform the data into useful information. He wants to know the top cost or expenses and whether his feeling they are out of control is justified and he wants to know the reasons for the top expenses, the tools he will use here are fishbone, pareto diagram, and graph.

Then, he wants to take some action by reducing the costs by 20% in the next 12 months so he wants to know where he should focus his cost reduction effort. The tools he wants to use are pareto again, and matrix diagram.

And finally, he wants to establish a cost control process to alert him when costs are spiraling out of control. He decides to use a control chart for this.

Now let's look at how he does.

Here is the 5W2H, he feels he can go deeper into the grasping the situation, but he knows this is a good start. So, he moves on to the next tool.

What: Checking account balance is low, overdraft sometimes
Why: Overspending, not keeping good accounting records
Where: Spending is spread over all areas
Who: College student
When: The last twelve months.
How: Buy whatever he needs or wants
How much: about $63,000 a year.

He draws a simple process chart to show how he is spending money now. He uses three methods to pay for the expenses, cash, credit card, and checks. To know the major expenses, he has to create a checksheet to transfer the data from these methods.

download data at this point

He uses an excel spreadsheet as a checksheet and transfers the data onto it for the last 12 months.

													Total
Haircuts	15	15	15	15	15	15	15	15	15	15	15	15	180
Shampoos	8	0	0	9	0	12	0	13	5	0	14	0	61
Massage/Spa	25	0	20	0	25	24	6	15	0	0	30	15	154
Pets food	20	24	30	12	15	23	10	14	0	15	24	23	210
Food	240	505	290	150	254	325	250	200	190	241	185	165	2795
Veterinary care	0	250	0	0	125	0	0	231	0	0	210	0	816
Coffees	125	85	90	180	145	105	104	156	142	120	141	104	1497
Pet sitter	75	65	75	75	75	75	60	65	60	75	75	75	850
Giving at Church	50	50	50	50	50	50	50	50	50	50	50	50	600
Donations to charities	0	125	0	240	0	0	300	0	125	250	200	300	1540
Car payments	450	450	450	450	450	450	450	450	450	450	450	450	5400
Gasoline	465	505	490	432	512	425	421	463	520	250	451	658	5592
Car insurance	150	150	150	150	150	150	150	150	150	150	150	150	1800
Car tolls	50	35	50	65	45	50	65	45	55	40	50	55	625
Income tax return	0	0	0	125	0	0	0	0	0	0	0	0	125
Gifts for parents	0	0	0	0	0	95	0	0	0	0	0	150	245
Gifts for siblings	125	0	240	0	210	0	0	250	263	210	0	0	1298
Eating out restaurants	560	650	210	150	525	480	421	356	754	451	210	853	5590
Birthday cards	25	0	0	53	0	0	14	0	21	12	25	20	170
Cleaning supplies	35	25	21	42	25	62	25	20	25	36	34	26	376
Kitchen ingredients	52	0	6	12	0	0	0	21	0	12	21	12	130
Bedding	0	0	0	53	0	0	0	0	25	0	0	0	78
Clothes	125	0	0	0	142	0	0	230	210	0	0	124	831
Yardcare	45	45	45	45	45	45	45	45	45	45	45	45	540
Tools	125	0	0	21	41	42	23	0	0	0	24	0	276
Doctor visits	0	250	0	0	230	240	0	0	0	0	435	210	1360
Dentist visits	2400	0	0	0	0	0	125	0	0	0	0	0	2525
Optometrist visits	0	0	0	0	220	0	0	0	0	0	0	0	220
Prescription drugs	0	45	0	52	0	56	0	65	0	45	0	54	317
Vitamins supplements	25	25	25	25	25	25	25	25	25	25	25	25	300
Gym	50	50	50	50	50	50	50	50	50	50	50	50	600
Professional society dues	125	0	0	0	0	0	0	0	0	0	0	0	125
Music	0	0	25	0	30	0	40	0	0	23	0	125	243
Books	25	0	0	0	51	0	0	0	56	0	132	0	264
TV subscriptions	125	125	125	125	125	125	125	125	125	125	125	125	1500
Phone fees	50	50	50	50	50	50	50	50	50	50	50	50	600
Wifi	25	25	25	25	25	25	25	25	25	25	25	25	300
Trips (vacations) airfare,h	1250	0	0	0	0	1320	0	0	0	0	0	2541	5111
Rents	1250	1250	1250	1250	1250	1250	1250	1250	1250	1250	1250	1250	15000
Water and utilities	52	54	32	54	50	56	50	54	52	49	48	45	596

He uses the graph function in excel and draws bar chart.

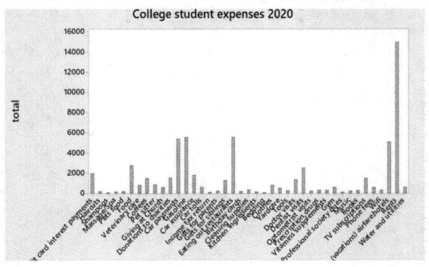

College student expenses 2020

7 and pie chart of the expenses.

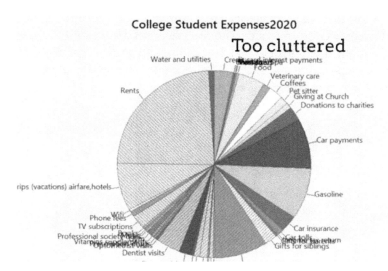

College Student Expenses2020

Too cluttered

The charts are too cluttered, so he uses an affinity diagram to group expenses and classify them into different categories. He wants to know the highest cost items, so he uses the total expenses instead of monthly expenses for now.

Personal		12369	Giving at Church	600	
Haircuts	180		Donations to charities	1540	
Shampoos	61				
Massage/Spa	154		Car		13417
Bedding	78		Car payments	5400	
Clothes	831		Gasoline	5592	
Doctor visits	1360		Car insurance	1800	
Dentist visits	2525		Car tolls	625	
Optometrist visits	220				
Prescription drugs	317		Household items		1192
Vitamins supplements	300		Cleaning supplies	376	
Gym	600		Yardcare	540	
Professional society dues	125		Tools	276	
Music	243				
Books	264		Rents		17996
Trips (vacations) airfare,hot	5111		Rents	15000	
			Water and utilities	596	
Credit card interest payment		1986	TV subscriptions	1500	
	1986		Phone fees	600	
Pets		1876	Wifi	300	
Pets food	210				
Veterinary care	816		Miscellaneous		1838
Pet sitter	850		Income tax return	125	
			Gifts for parents	245	
Food		10012	Gifts for siblings	1298	
Food	2795		Birthday cards	170	
Coffees	1497				

He then reruns the bar chart and pie chart with the categorical data instead of itemized data. The top expenses are easier to see. He can see the highest expense is rent and the next highest is car and personal but car and personal are so close, so he wants to know which one is really second highest expense.

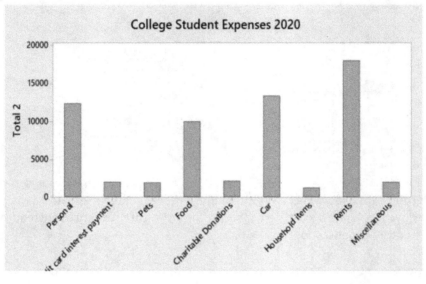

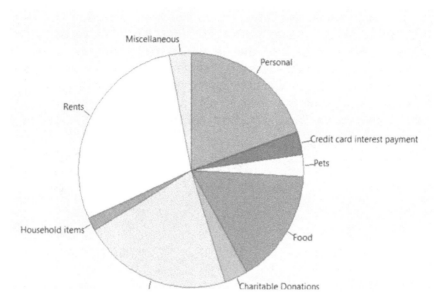

So, he uses pareto using the data from the checksheet. But he quickly sees that this chart is too busy.

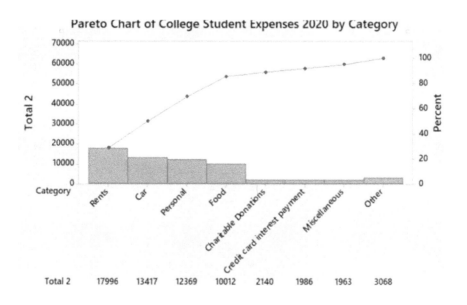

So, he uses the categories of expenses instead, and now the pareto is easier to see. and this chart shows car is the second highest expense. He goes back to the itemized list of expenses for car and personal and sees that these are needed expenses, he can try to cut these expenses, but he wants to look at the next opportunity and try to see any low hanging fruit for cost reduction. He looks at food which is forth highest bar and is 15.9% of total expense.

Personal		12369
Haircuts	180	
Shampoos	61	
Massage/Spa	154	
Bedding	78	
Clothes	831	
Doctor visits	1360	
Dentist visits	2525	
Optometrist visits	220	
Prescription drugs	317	
Vitamins supplements	300	
Gym	600	
Professional society dues	125	
Music	243	
Books	264	
Trips (vacations) airfare,hot	5111	
Credit card interest payment		1986
	1986	
Pets		1876
Pets food	210	
Veterinary care	816	
Pet sitter	850	
Food		10012
Food	2795	
Coffees	1497	

Giving at Church	600	
Donations to charities	1540	
Car		13417
Car payments	5400	
Gasoline	5592	
Car insurance	1800	
Car tolls	625	
Household items		1192
Cleaning supplies	376	
Yardcare	540	
Tools	276	
Rents		17996
Rents	15000	
Water and utilities	596	
TV subscriptions	1500	
Phone fees	600	
Wifi	300	
Miscellaneous		1838
Income tax return	125	
Gifts for parents	245	
Gifts for siblings	1298	
Birthday cards	170	

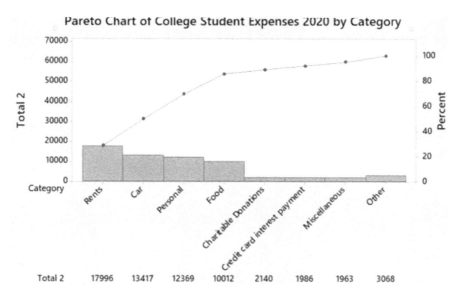

Pareto Chart of College Student Expenses 2020 by Category

Total 2	17996	13417	12369	10012	2140	1986	1963	3068

He went back to the food category and sees that the biggest amount in this category is eating out which totaled 5,590 last year.

Personal		12369
Haircuts	180	
Shampoos	61	
Massage/Spa	154	
Bedding	78	
Clothes	831	
Doctor visits	1360	
Dentist visits	2525	
Optometrist visits	220	
Prescription drugs	317	
Vitamins supplements	300	
Gym	600	
Professional society dues	125	
Music	243	
Books	264	
Trips (vacations) airfare,hot	5111	
Credit card interest payment		1986
	1986	
Pets		1876
Pets food	210	
Veterinary care	816	
Pet sitter	850	
Food		10012
Food	2795	
Coffees	1497	

Giving at church		600
Donations to charities	1540	
Car		13417
Car payments	5400	
Gasoline	5592	
Car insurance	1800	
Car tolls	625	
Household items		1192
Cleaning supplies	376	
Yardcare	540	
Tools	276	
Rents		17996
Rents	15000	
Water and utilities	596	
TV subscriptions	1500	
Phone fees	600	
Wifi	300	
Miscellaneous		1838
Income tax return	125	
Gifts for parents	245	
Gifts for siblings	1298	
Birthday cards	170	

He uses a line chart to see his eating out pattern. The chart shows December, November and February are the three months with highest expenses of eating out. He wants to analyze this data by using a fishbone.

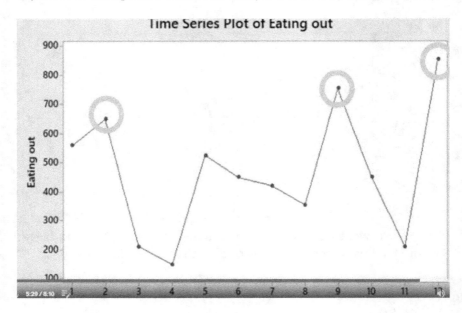

He brainstorms and tries to recall any special events during those three months that might have caused him to eat out. He captures these data on the fishbone chart, but he couldn't find anything special from the fishbone.

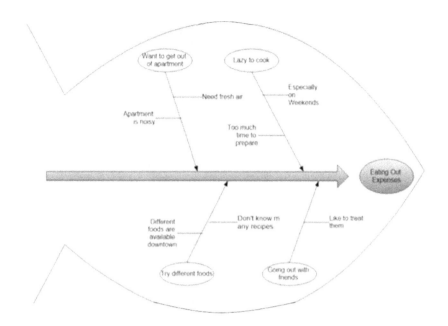

So, he decides to go back and looks at the top categories of expenses which are rent, car, personal and food. He sets a goal to reduce the expenses by 20% next year so he wants to know where he should focus his effort and by how much. He spent 62,951 in 2020 and 20% less will give him a budget of 49,500. First he looks rents, there is nothing he can do here unless moving to a cheaper apartment which he does want to do yet. next car category, he wants to use car less therefore less gasoline so he wants to cut 6.3 % here or 3,966, next personal category, he will reduce vacation trips and can save 7.6% or 5,316, and finally food, he will eat out less and eat more healthy foods and this should reduce doctor visits, and he will make his own coffee. He thinks he can reduce it by 6.9% or 4,344. When the total goes up the saving it comes out to be 20.8% or 0.8% higher than target but he wants to keep it as contingency.

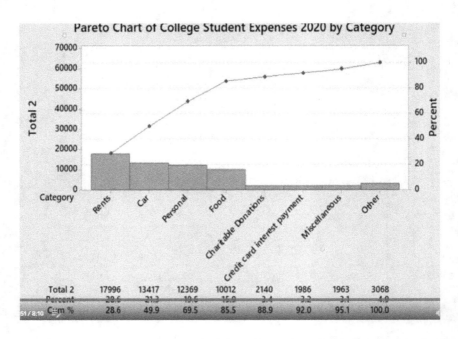

Being a data engineer, he updates his checksheet to include target for 2021 and monthly average for all four categories above. Usually this would be enough to control expenses, but he wants to apply the most powerful tool in his toolbox, the control charts.

He wants to reduce expenses by 20% in the next 12 months 2021

	2020	2021	%reduce	$reduce	Remarks
Total expenses	62,951	49,600	20%	12,590	
Rents	28.6%	28.6%	0.0%	$0	no change to rent
Car	21.3%	15.0%	6.3%	$3,966	Less use of car , save on gasoline
Personal	19.6%	12.0%	7.6%	$5,316	Reduce vacations/trips
Food	15.9%	9.0%	6.9%	$4,344	Less eating out, eat more healthy foods, reduce doctor visits, make own coffee
Target top four categories on pareto charts			20.8%		

146

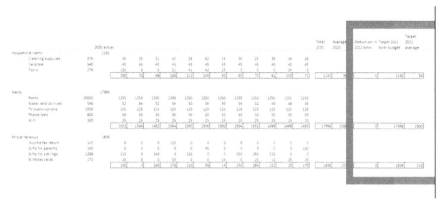

So he draws three control charts for the three top expenses using the twelve months in 2020 to calculate control limits and means. Here are the control charts. Looking at these control charts, he knows the most challenging expense is car. Do you know why this is the case? please see the explanation in the small box on the right side of the chart.

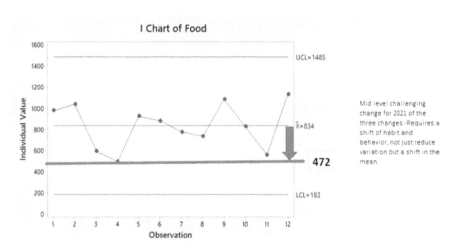

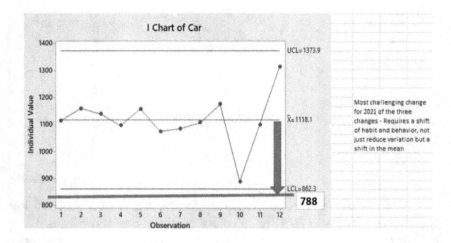

To wrap this up, he uses the process diagram to standardize his new spending pattern and he creates this with the process chart tool.

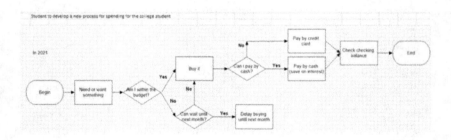

4.2 Synthesis Method 2: Descriptive, Predictive, Prescriptive

The second method is the descriptive to preventive approach. This method groups tools into the intended functions they perform. The descriptive method explains what happened. This includes Key Process Indicators or KPIs and the corresponding metrics that tell us something has occurred, collection of data, processing of data, data analysis and visualization, and insights into past performance, all related to describing the situation or the problem. Tools used for descriptive functions include process flow diagrams, checksheets, histograms, charts, affinity diagrams, and spaghetti diagrams.

Descriptive (what happened?)	Diagnostic (Why and how did it happen?)	Predictive (What and when will it happen?)	Prescriptive (What should be done reactively?)	Preventive (What should be done proactively?)
KPI Metrics Data collection Data processing Data analysis Data visualization Insights of past performance	Root cause Statistical analysis Trends Relationships	Machine learning Strategies Patterns in datasets	Checklist Diagnostics Standard countermeasures	Risk analysis Problem prevention Process planning
Process flow diagram Checksheets Histograms Charts Affinity diagrams Spaghetti diagrams Pareto	Cause and effect diagram Scatter diagrams Matrix diagrams C-E matrix	Scatter diagrams Histograms Pareto diagrams Charts Matrix diagrams C-E matrix	Pareto diagrams Charts Matrix diagrams C-E matrix PDPC Process flow	Control charts Charts Matrix diagrams C-E matrix PDPC

The diagnostic approach is telling people why and how things happened. It involves breaking the problem down and looking at it in detail. Here finding root cause, doing statistical analysis, trends, relationships between variables bring light into the problem being investigated. Tools used include cause and effect diagram, scatter diagram, matrix diagrams and Cause and effect matrix.

The predictive approach is an attempt to say what will happen. This is based on data collected and analyzed. Here different machine learning strategies, and patterns in datasets can reveal with statistical confidence the likelihood of occurrence of an event. Here tools such as scatter diagram, histograms, pareto diagrams, charts, matrix diagrams, Cause and effect matrix and affinity diagram can help. There are advanced statistical tools that are used in this approach.

The prescriptive approach is used to answer the question; what should be done? when a problem or a situation is at hand. The best method is to learn from past experience as in Lessons Learned of previous situations of similar nature. However, lacking the previous experience, tools such as Pareto diagram, charts, matrix diagrams, cause and effect matrix, process decision program chart can be used.

Finally, a preventive approach is used proactively during review sessions of similar situations or projects to prevent the same problem from occurring. Tools such as control charts, charts, matrix diagrams and cause and effect matrix are used.

In this section, we will show examples of tools synthesized by the five functions they perform. Descriptive, Diagnostic, predictive, prescriptive, and preventive. Descriptive tools define the problem and describe what happened by using Key Performance indicators or KPI, metrics for measurement, collection of data, processing data, data analysis, data visualization and insights into past performance. Tools used include process flow diagram, checksheet, histograms, charts, affinity diagram, and spaghetti diagrams.

Diagnostic tools explain why things happened? here finding root cause, doing statistical analysis, studying trends, relationships. Tools used include cause and effect diagram, scatter diagram, matrix diagram and Cause and effect matrix.

Predictive tools forecast what will happen? They are machine learning, strategies, and patterns in datasets. Tools used include scatter diagram, pareto diagram, charts, matrix diagrams, Cause and effect matrix and affinity diagram. You can see some tools perform multiple functions.

Prescriptive tools help define what should be done? Here problems have already occurred, and prescriptive tools used past data to do their jobs. Tools include pareto diagram, charts, matrix diagram, cause and effect matrix and process decision program chart.

Preventive tools help define what should be done proactively to prevent problems from occurring. The difference between predictive and preventive is predictive predicts statistically the probability of something to happen, preventive is to reduce the chance of occurring or prevent it from happening completely. Tools used include control charts, charts, matrix diagrams, Cause and effect matrix and Process decision program chart.

Here is an example of a situation and the tools used to solve the problem. The situation is a toy company is suffering from customer complaints. The owner wants to know why the customers are returning goods. The company data analysis wants to use checksheet, pareto and graph.

Example 2: A CEO of a toy company wants to improve quality of toys				
Descriptive (what happened?)	Diagnostic (Why and how did it happen?)	Predictive (What and when will it happen?)	Prescriptive (What should be done reactively?)	Preventive (What should be done proactively?)
A toy company is suffering from customer complaints. The owner wants to know why the customers are returning goods.	The owner of the above company wants to know the causes of the problems	The same owner wants to know how many products are going to be returned in the next month	The owner want to have a plan to address each customer problem effectively	He wants to have a method to know if the new product is going to be received well. If not, what does he need to do now?
Checksheet Histograms Charts Pareto	Cause and effect diagram	Histograms	Process flow	Control charts Charts

Descriptive

Situation:

A toy company is suffering from customer complaints. The owner wants to know why the customers are returning goods.

The same owner of the above company wants to know the causes of the problems. The diagnostic tool the data analysis wants to use is fishbone.

The owner then wants to know how many products are going to be returned in the next months. The data analysis wants to use histogram.

The owner wants to have a plan to address each customer's problem effectively. The data analysis uses a process map and Process Decision program chart or PDPC.

The company is developing new toys, the owner wants to know if the new toy is going to be received well. If not, what does he need to do. The data analysis uses control charts and graphs.

Here are the results of the data analysis work.

Descriptive tools. The situation is written down and the picture of the toy is attached.

Descriptive. He Creates a checksheet to collect data. The data analysis looks at all returns in the month of January 2021 and tallies the quantity by types of problems. There are 59 returns for one month. Step 2. He creates a pareto chart that shows the number one problem is tire came off rim which is 33. 9 % of all return for that month.

Toy Name : Remote control toy cars
Return month: January 2021
Return qu Reason

5	Car not working
15	Remote control not working
20	Tire came off rim
3	Smell smoke
15	Noise and rattles
1	Others
59	Total

Step 2 - Pareto chart

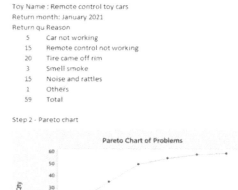

He compares the data to last year's return of the same time frame January 2021 to January 2020 and finds this year return is almost triple. He is done with the descriptive using the three tools of checksheet, pareto and bar chart. He now moves to diagnostic tools.

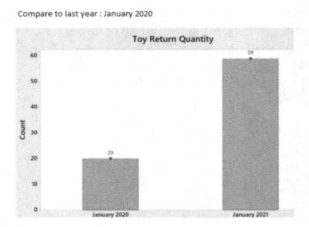

The owner wants to know the causes of returns, so the data analysis uses the fishbone and transfers customers' complaints onto the chart to find the causes of the highest return which is tires come off the rim. He will use more fishbone diagrams for other defects but for now he remains with the highest complaint. The fishbone indicates that tires are oversized as a sure cause due to many complaints from customers.

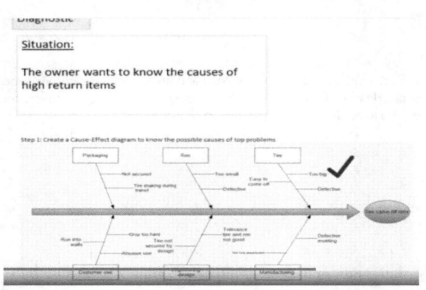

154

He creates a Cause effect matrix and looks at all 20 return tires. Here is the breakdown of the causes of tire come off rim. He confirmed all 10 big tires and found they are all out of spec. The drawing indicates the max tire diameter is 1.7 inches and the 10 return tires measure from 1.8 to 2.1.

Step 2: Create a matrix to correlate causes and effects

Examining the defective toys, the following matrix is formed

Defects	Tire too big	Rim too small	Damaged (packaging	Damaged (abusive u	Unknown	Total
Tire come off rim	10	5	2	2	1	20

Measure the tire diameter and drawing
Diameter measurements (in inches)

1.9	1.9
1.8	2.1
1.8	1.8
1.9	1.8
2	1.9

Drawing
Tire diameter 1.5+0.2/-0.2
Max 1.7
Min 1.3

He now moves to the predictive tool because the owner wants to know how many products will be returned next month. He knows that tire size is a cause of returns, so he randomly measures 160 tires of the same lot as those sold but not yet returned. he plots the data using histogram and He finds that 15% of the 160 samples are too big.

Situation:

The owner wants to know how many products will be returned in the next month

Step 1: Use histogram to estimate the percent defective of tire
Take 160 tires and measure the tires, the following histogram is created

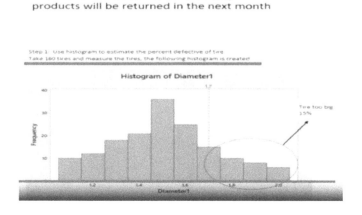

Histogram of Diameter1

Tire too big
15%

Now he has to estimate the total rejects for next month, so he looks at the record and finds that 1000 toys of the same model were sold in January 2021 and the total reject for January is 59 toys or 5.9%. If nothing is changed, he expects the same rejects percent will be for the future. However, he knows that 33.9% of the rejections are due to tire problems. He calculates the total rejections due to tire by multiplying 5.9% with 33.9% and gets 2% which is the total rejections of the cars due to tire problems. So, he proposes to the owner to sort all tires in stock and use only good ones and the predicted rejection will be reduced from 5.9% to 3.9%.

He now moves to prescriptive tools and answers the question the owner has: he wants to have a plan to address each customer's problem effectively. The data analysis creates a process decision program chart to assess risks and countermeasures. On the left side is the process of building the toy cars. It has three main elements: Receive parts from suppliers such as tires, motors, the potential problems are parts out of specification. risk is high because customer complaints and return products, so the countermeasure is to measure all tires and rims for correct dimensions at suppliers as certified stocks. They will not use any parts without this certification.

Prescriptive

Situation:

The owner wants to have a plan to address each customer problem effectively

Step 1: Create a Process Decision Program chart to assess risks and countermeasures

Process Elements	Potential Problems	Risk	Countermeasures
1. Receive parts from suppliers, tires, motors, etc.	Parts out of specifications or damaged	High	Measure all tires and rims for correct dimensions
2. Assembly parts	Wrong parts installed	Low	Visual display the standards
3. Inspection finished products before shipping	Some functions may not work	Low	Make a list of customers conern items and inspect the products

The second process element is assembly parts. The potential problems here are wrong parts installed by the assemblers. The risk is low wrong parts are identified with labels; the assemblers are trained to use the right parts. The countermeasures are display visual standards to remind the assembler of the correct parts.

The third process element is inspection of finished products before shipping. The potential problem here is that some functions may not work as a finished product. The risk is low because there are some function checks being done already but not all. The countermeasure is to list the customer concern items and improve the final check of the products. There are many other countermeasures that can be done such as error proofing or mistake proofing, but the owner is satisfied with this plan for now.

Next the data analysis moves to the preventive and tries to answer the owner's mandate to have a method to know if the product is to be received well, if not what does he need to do. This is to protect the brand image.

Preventive

Situation:

The owner wants to have a method to know if the new product is going to be received well. If not, what does he need to do?

The data analysis uses the PDPC he put together previously and creates a process flow diagram for the owner's operations manager. The owner is satisfied with this method, but he wants to have a report from the operations manager about the operations before the customers complain.

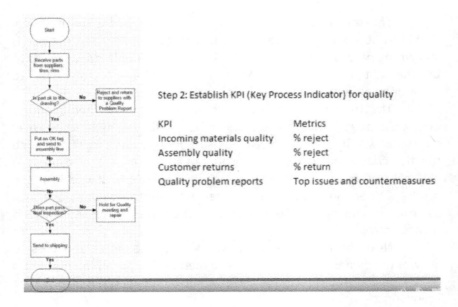

Step 2: Establish KPI (Key Process Indicator) for quality

KPI	Metrics
Incoming materials quality	% reject
Assembly quality	% reject
Customer returns	% return
Quality problem reports	Top issues and countermeasures

So, the data analysis creates a list of KPI or key performance indicators for the operations manager to use to report out each month to the owner. He attaches the control charts for each KPI.

4.3 Synthesis Method 3: Others

The third synthesis method of tools is grouping tools according to the type of data. Tools are best used when data are presented in a certain way. The first way is Trends or variations. Tools such as time series charts, run charts, control charts have X axis as time. They show how data vary over time and from this variation, decisions are made.

Trend (Variations)	Distribution (Patterns)	Relationship (Comparison)
Time series charts Run charts Control charts	Histograms Dot plots (individual plots) Box plots Pareto diagrams Charts	Cause and effect diagram Cause and effect matrix Scatter diagram Relations diagram Affinity diagram Matrix data Systematic diagram Arrow diagram

The second way is distribution or patterns of data. Charts, scatter diagrams, histograms present individual data and how they relate to the larger group of data or sample and population.

The third way is relationships or comparison of variables. Histograms, charts, cause and effect diagram, cause and effect matrix, pareto diagram show the relative magnitudes of variable among others.

So, you can see the 17 tools you will learn in this book will help you tackle all sorts of problems and situations.

In this section, you will learn the third method of synthesizing the tools according to basic statistics. This method is about using the right tool for the right purpose such as choosing the correct visuals in power Bi.

Tools are a means to an end. There are three ends in showing data. The trends showing variations over time, the distributions showing the patterns and the relationships showing the comparative values between variables.

For trends, time series charts, run chart and control charts, all three uses time as the X coordinate and the values of the characteristics as the Y coordinate.

For distribution, histogram, dot plot or individual plot, box plot, pareto and charts show the distributions or pattern of sample data. This is used widely in estimating the population values using statistics.

For relationships of variables, Cause and effect diagram and matrix, scatter diagram, relations diagram, affinity diagram, matrix data, systematic diagram or tree diagram and arrow diagram show the relationships between variables.

Trend (Variations)	Distribution (Patterns)	Relationship (Comparison)
Covid new cases	Market share of smart phones in France	What are the relationships between happiness and affected factors
Charts Graphs	Histograms	Relation diagrams

There are numerous examples on the internet. Here are three examples. For trends covid new cases in the US using time series line chart. For distributions, the market share of smart phones in France using histogram, and finally, the relationship between happiness and affected factors using relations diagram is shown.

Here is an example of a trend chart of covid new cases in the US. New cases are shown in the bar chart and line chart is shown using 7-day average to smooth out the sharp daily changes. Information that can be obtained from trend charts is slope of trends, max values, and current status. We can see the trend of daily infection is increasing.

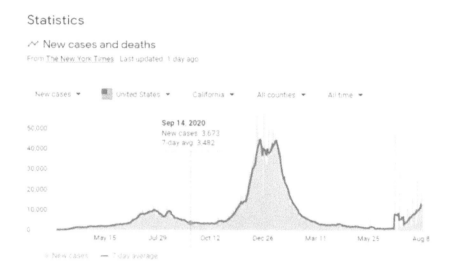

Here is the example of the distribution of smart phone market share in France. iPhone 11 is 11% of total market share and is the highest of all brands. If all three iPhone 11 models are combined, iPhone 11 occupies 25% of total market share.

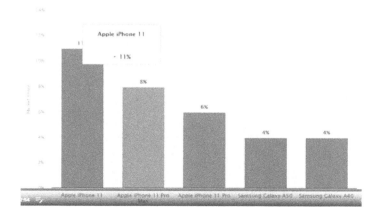

And here is an example of the relations between variables method using relation diagram. Here is what people say in a survey about what affects their happiness. All six categories affect happiness.

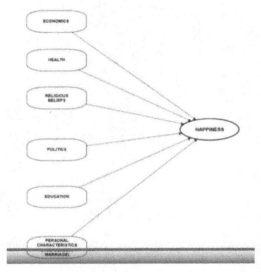

4.4 Quiz 4: Test Your Knowledge

Question 1:

The correct synthesis of tools for continuous improvement or problem solving is :

○ Check sheet, line chart, cause and effect, control charts

○ 5W2H, check sheet, charts, pareto, cause and effect, matrix, control charts

○ Affinity diagram, check sheet, pareto, arrow diagram, control charts

Question 2:

Is Predictive and Preventive the same?

○ Yes, they are similar

○ No , predictive is not the same as preventive

How many ways are data usually shown ?

○ Many ways, not a fixed number

○ Three ways, past, present, future

○ Three ways, trends, distributions, relationships

Appendix

Appendix 1: Answers to Quizzes

Question 1:

Why the adage "Data is Truth!" is not always true?

○ Data contains errors

○ Data is only reflecting a small sample

○ Data can be interpreted wrong

○ Data can be manipulated

◉ **All of the above**

Question 2:

Why do we need the right tools for data analysis ?

○ So that errors can be avoided

○ To build a good dashboard

◉ **To convert data into useful information**

○ To maximize use of data

Appendix 1: Answers to quizzes

Question 3:

What is the purpose of synthesizing tools?

○ To use the right tools for the right purpose

○ To maximize the benefits of tools

○ To show the logic of arriving at a conclusion

● All of the above

Question 4:

Is checksheet used for tally count only?

○ Yes.

● No, Checksheet can be used for any type of data.

Question 5:

Is Pareto the same as bar chart with bars arranged from highest to lowest frequency? dick

○ Yes, they are the same only with bars re-arranged. The

○ No, they are different because Pareto diagram follows the 80/20 rules

● No, they are different because Pareto diagram has percent cumulative line.

Appendix 1: Answers to quizzes

Question 1:

Grasping the situation is necessary before diving into the problem because:

○ **The problem is not always where it appears to be.**

○ **To avoid quick judgment which can lead to wrong solution.**

○ **The symptom may be the same as before but the root cause may be different**

○ **time and effort can be wasted if attacking the wrong problem**

● **All of the above**

Question 2:

Is Spaghetti diagram one of the 7 traditional QC tools?

○ **Yes**

● **No, it is not**

Question 3:

Does the fishbone chart have 6 main causes: Man, Machine, Method, Materials, Measurement, Environment. ?

○ **Yes, this is traditional accepted practice**

● **No, it can have other causes.**

Appendix 1: Answers to quizzes

Question 4:

How many data points does histogram diagram require ?

○ **50 data points**

○ **100 data points**

○ **150 data points**

● **20 data points or more**

Question 5:

What is the tool to use to study relationship between two variables ?

○ **Pareto diagram**

● **Scatter diagram**

○ **Bar chart**

○ **Histogram**

Question 6:

Does fishbone diagram list only known causes?

○ **Yes**

● **No**

Appendix 1: Answers to quizzes

Question 7:

Is run chart the same as line chart?

○ **Yes, they are the same**

● **No, run chart is used to study if special cause exists while line chart is used to study variation**

Question 8:

What are control limits on control charts?

● **They are limits calculated from process variation to show if process is operating normal or abnormal**

○ **They are the same as specification limits**

○ **They are the same as control plans**

○ **They are the same as max and min lines**

Question 9:

Are two variables plotted on scatter diagram always causes and effect ?

○ **Yes**

● **No**

○ **Three pairs**

Appendix 1: Answers to quizzes

Question 10:

How many frequency bars are required for histogram?

○ 2

○ 3

○ 4

○ 5 or more

● **It depends on number of data points**

Question 1:

Is Cause and Effect matrix similar to Cause and Effect diagram?

○ Yes because they study causes and effects

○ No, because one is matrix and the other is a diagram

● **No, because cause and effect matrix can study many effects and many causes at the same time, while cause and effect diagram studies only one effect and many causes**

Question 2:

How many components does Affinity diagram have ?

○ One, the Headers

● **Two, the Headers and the Ideas**

○ Three, the Headers, Ideas and Analysis

Appendix 1: Answers to quizzes

Question 3:

What tool is used to study complex relationships between many variables initially?

○ Systematic diagram

○ Affinity diagram

● Relations diagram

○ Matrix diagram

○ Arrow diagram

Question 4:

What are the main indicators for arrow diagram?

● Critical path and resources

○ Resources and number of activities

○ Critical path

Question 5:

What tool is used to assess risks ?

○ Relations diagram

○ Affinity diagram

● Process Decision Program Chart (PDPC)

○ Matrix data analysis

Appendix 1: Answers to quizzes

Question 6:

What is the difference between errors and lies ?

⬤ **Errors are interpreting charts wrongly because lack of knowledge, Lies are interpreting charts wrongly because the person wants to deceive the readers of the charts.**

○ **Errors are poor judgments, lies are withholding correct judgments**

○ **Errors are when the mind sees reality not correctly, lies are when the mind sees reality correctly but the person says something different**

Question 7:

Is Tree diagram the same as 5 Why's?

⬤ **Yes, both are systematic diagrams**

○ **No, Tree diagram is systematic diagram, 5 Why's is root cause analysis**

○ **No, Tree diagram is horizontal, 5Why's is vertical**

Question 1:

The correct synthesis of tools for continuous improvement or problem solving is :

○ **Check sheet, line chart, cause and effect, control charts**

⬤ **5W2H, check sheet, charts, pareto, cause and effect, matrix, control charts**

○ **Affinity diagram, check sheet, pareto, arrow diagram, control charts**

Question 2:

Is Predictive and Preventive the same?

○ **Yes, they are similar**

⬤ **No , predictive is not the same as preventive**

Appendix 1: Answers to quizzes

How many ways are data usually shown ?

○   **Many ways, not a fixed number**

○   **Three ways, past, present, future**

●   **Three ways, trends, distributions, relationships**

Appendix 2: Resource Table

	Tools	Purpose	When to use	How to Use	Examples of Use
	5W2H	To grasp the situation, gather all relevant data from a wide perspective to know everything about the situation	No background is given and limited information is available to begin an investigation	Ask What happened, Where, Why, When, Who and How and How much to gather data	Why the customers are rejecting products
	Process Flow(flow chart)	Assemble the elements and sequence of work to be performed to produce a product or service Visually see who does what (Swim lanes for responsible persons: person to person flowchart)	Find where a cause of a problem resides, Opportunities for improvement,How things are made,How much time it takes to do something,How can things be done faster,Where the weak links are	Start and end pointsfill in the middle with events or actions Use symbols: process, decision, data, document, storage, use arrows to connect the elements	How to cook or bake a cake How to do something
	Checksheets	To collect and organize facts and data Use checklist as checksheets if check items are known and repetitive Locations of incidents: Location checksheet	To know quantitatively and qualitatively about something To establish baseline for improvement To communicate accurately what we mean Make better decisions Solve problems faster	Know type of data to be collected: Continuous, Discrete, Locations. Counted data: use tick marks, also called tally . Individual measurement: use numerical data Break down by shift, day, month	Count number of people entering restaurants Count number of cars travelling on road Weights and heights of children growth
	Graphs	To display data in understandable formats	To draw conclusion about the data to make decision To see trends, patterns descriptively To predict the future using past data To see behavior over time	Kinds of graphs and usage:Line chart Bar chart Pie chart, donut chart Stacked bar chart Area chart Water fall chart Tree map Gantt Chart Radar chart Heat map Dot plot Spaghetti chart	Trends of sales of iphone products, college graduates by university
	Cause and Effect	To find the cause of a problem ,Generate possible causes to solve a particular problem	To know the cause instead of symptoms,To know what drives the changes or variations,To cover all possible causes	Brainstorming to generate ideas,Prioritizing: Affect, not affect, not sure,Test the relationship cause and effect	High traffic accidents at the intersection

Appendix 2 - Resource Table

	Tools	Purpose	When to use	How to Use	Examples of Use
	Scatter Diagram (correlation chart)	To see the relationship between two different variables	How much one thing affect the other,What things affect the outcome or results,Use the familiar variable to know the unfamiliar variables,check real cause and effect	Plot the data in pairs (x,y chart),Visually check for correlation (a line) or not (bundle),Check for cause-effect relationship,Relationship between one cause and another cause,Relationship between one cause and two other causes	Temperature affect length of pipe
	Histograms	To see how often (frequency) something occurs comparing to others	Top or bottom percent of a group of something,Are there any grouping of data and what they look like,Want to know how data are distributed (bell curve)	Use 50 to 100 data points,Data points fall within certain interval or bars,The frequency of data is the height of histogram for that bar,if normally distributed, can predict the performance	Population of a city based on age, education
	Control charts	To know if the data is just natural variation or something external causes disturbs it	Analyze the variation in a process,Use to make decision to take action to correct or let it run,Predict percent of bad products produced and when,Know if process improvement is real	Use I-MR chart if data is counted individually,(most cost effective chart, easy to use),Use Xbar-R chart if data are calculated in sub-groups,(more accurate of predicting process behavior)	Energy use (Electricity),Gasoline consumptions (miles driven before fill up)
	Pareto Diagram	To know the critical few from the trivial many (greatest contributions),To prioritize	What are the critical few things that affect most,(80/20 rule)	Collect data in bar chart, frequency of event occurences,Arrange bar with highest frequency first,Cascade to lowest frequency,Calculate the cummulative frequency	Top companies with highest market caps
	Matrix Diagrams (C-E Matrix)	Summarize and organize data into rows and columns to see the relationships between them	What are the actions for corresponding problems,To know the strength of the relationships between variables by assigning a numerical value (3,2,1) at intersections	Many types of matrix: L, T, X, Y, C,Data have common columns and rows	Demographic data of Gen X regarding purchasing power

174

Appendix 2 - Resource Table

	Tools	Purpose	When to use	How to Use	Examples of Use
	Tree diagram	From an objective, generate all possible details to accomplish the objective. Objective is the trunk details are the roots. The trunk is goal, roots are means. Or trunk is why, roots are how	cascade top goals to lower levels in an organization to implement Develop different sub-systems to meet the system function Break a complex problem into simple ones	Determine the goal, generate first level how First level how's are now goals, generate second level hows continue the cascade	Brake failure
	Spaghetti diagram	Spaghetti diagram is used to describe the flow of material, people or information in any situation.	Spaghetti diagram visually displays the flows so that the points of cause of problems can be seen and improvement made. Delivery of materials, people walking in the factories of offices,	Draw strings to simulate the flows of materials, people and information. Trace the beginnings and ends of strings for each trip	Study the walks of people in an office or factory
	Affinity diagram	Affinity diagram is tool to organize data, facts, information, opinions into groups of similar topics or themes	Where there are many ideas but unorganized. It means bring chaos into order	Affinity diagram has only two main components: ideas and idea headers. brain storming to generate ideas. Once ideas are generated, they are organized into headers as shown.	Traits of olympic atheletes in swimming events
	Relations diagram	Relations diagram is free thinking technique and the scope is broad in finding many causes and many effects	relations diagram is used for more complex situations with many scattered issues where cause and effect cannot be established easily.	Begins with a situation. Free thinking will generate relevant ideas dispersed throughout the page. When a cause and effect relationship between two elements is recognized, an arrow is drawn with the arrow pointing to the effect.	What makes a billionaire?
	Arrow diagram (Activity Network Diagram)	Arrow diagram or activity network diagram manages tasks in a project graphically where the relationships and orders between tasks must be maintained so that problems with scheduling, resources are addressed and solutions provided	Used to control schedules and for estimating the best way to complete the entire project	Each activity has a duration time, then, link up all these activities by arrows in the sequence of occuring, either in series of one another or in parallel of one another. Then determine the critical path.	Building a bridge in Alaska

Appendix 2 - Resource Table

	Tools	Purpose	When to use	How to Use	Examples of Use
	Process Decision Program Chart (PDPC)	PDPC, determines the process to be used and systematically identifies what could go wrong so that desired results could be achieved	PDPC deals with risks and countermeasures for each element of the process	Start with a process with actions to meet an objective. For each action element in the process, identify what could go wrong, these are risks to be addressed. Address each risk with countermeasures.	Launching a human cargo to space station
	Matrix Data Analysis	Matrix data analysis arranges data in a matrix form for ease of visualization and understanding	It is used when a set of variables behaving similarly within two identified characteristics are plotted on a X-Y chart.	To construct this matrix data analysis plot, start with a checksheet with column for variables, characteristic 1, and for characteristic 2. Once the data are collected, they are plotted on a X-Y graph	suburban dwellers and commutes

www.ingramcontent.com/pod-product-compliance
Lightning Source LLC
La Vergne TN
LVHW051236050326
832903LV00028B/2432